ROGER MANVELL

Shakespeare and the Film

with 48 pages of plates

LONDON
J. M. DENT & SONS LTD

First published 1971

© Text, Roger Manvell, 1971

Made in Great Britain
at the
Aldine Press · Letchworth · Herts
for
J. M. DENT & SONS LTD
Aldine House · Bedford Street · London

ISBN 0 460 03944 x

Contents

Illustrations

Acknowledgments

I should like to thank the following for the generous help they have given me in the course of the preparation of this book:

Laurence Irving for providing designs and information about the Fairbanks' production of *The Taming of the Shrew* (1929);

William Dieterle and Heinrich Fraenkel for information about the film versions of *A Midsummer Night's Dream* (1934);

Lord Olivier for information connected with his Shakespearean film productions;

Grigori Kozintsev for providing stills and information connected with his films of *Hamlet* and *King Lear*, and Miss Jeanne Beng for help with translation from the Russian;

Akira Kurosawa and Tadao Sato for information connected with the Japanese *Macbeth* (*The Castle of the Spider's Web*; *The Throne of Blood*);

Peter Hall for information about his film version of *A Midsummer Night's Dream*;

Lord Birkett and Peter Brook for information about their film production of *King Lear*, and for permission to quote from the advance script of the film.

Also my gratitude to the Society of Film and Television Arts for permission to reproduce material which has appeared in its Journal, and the editors of *Sight and Sound* and *Films and Filming* for permission to quote from articles appearing in their pages. I am indebted to the officers of the British Film Institute Information and Library departments for the help they have given, and to the Stills department for help in collecting the stills reproduced in this book. I am grateful to Mrs Enid Audus for typing the book.

I should like to acknowledge the help of the following companies in providing stills:

M.G.M.	Lenfilm
Warner Brothers	Sovexport Film
The Rank Organisation	Contemporary Films Ltd
Independent Film Distributors	Commonwealth United
Republic Pictures	Paramount Pictures
British Lion Films Ltd	Columbia Pictures Corporation
United Artists	BHE Productions
Academy Cinema	Eagle Films Ltd
Planet Films	Bargate Films
Hunter Films Ltd	

ROGER MANVELL

TO LAURENCE OLIVIER
whose Shakespearean films in
the 1940s first revealed the true
potentialities of Shakespeare on
the screen

Introduction

The purpose of this book is to describe and discuss the principal sound films which have been adapted from Shakespeare's plays, using either the original text or some form of close translation. With substantial help from the film-makers themselves, I hope to show how the plays have been presented to make them effective as films, and how the technique of the film itself has to be modified considerably to make it effective as a medium for Shakespeare, more especially if Shakespeare's verse is to become living, dramatic speech for film audiences.

Although some four hundred films were freely adapted from Shakespeare's plays during the period of the silent cinema, fewer than fifty have been produced so far during the sound period, some of the most remarkable in Russian and Japanese translations. The smallness of the number of adaptations is largely due to the high cost of full-scale production, which normally exceeds audience demand for Shakespearean films—though this situation has been changing in recent years with the growing demand of television for films of this kind. We can therefore expect that the number of Shakespearean films may well increase considerably in the future.

A few outstanding directors have used situations in the plays as sources from which to draw either period or modern 'parallels' for their screenplays—for example, Ernst Lubitsch in *To Be or not to Be* (1941), André Cayatte in *Les Amants de Vérone* (1948), Peter Ustinov in *Romanoff and Juliet* (1960), Robert Wise in the Jerome Robbins, Leonard Bernstein and Arthur Laurents musical, *West Side Story* (1961), Claude Chabrol in *Ophélia* (1962) and Andrzej Wajda in *The Siberian Lady Macbeth* (1961). These are not Shakespearean films, of course, and they are not discussed in this book, any more than ballets or operas derived from the plays are discussed in books about Shakespeare. Perhaps some may regard Akira Kurosawa's version of

Macbeth called *The Castle of the Spider's Web* (*The Throne of Blood*) as in this class of remote adaptations; it is included here because many film-makers, like myself, consider it to be one of the finest, and most exact in spirit, of the screen adaptations from Shakespeare. I have, however, omitted discussion of Jiri Trnka's feature-length puppet version of *A Midsummer Night's Dream* (1959), a fantasia remarkable more for its over-elaborate design and virtuosity in animation techniques than as a serious interpretation of Shakespeare's play.

Of the films discussed, there is only one I have not been able to see at the time of writing; Grigori Kozintsev's *King Lear* (1970). The information about this film, which promises us so much, was sent to me by Mr Kozintsev just after he had completed the film.

ROGER MANVELL

June 1971

NOTE. At the time of going to press, two Shakespearean films are in production: Roman Polanski's *Macbeth*, with Jon Finch and Francesca Annis as Macbeth and Lady Macbeth, and Charlton Heston's production, which he directs, of *Antony and Cleopatra*, with himself as Antony and Hildegard Neil as Cleopatra. Among other films in prospect is Michael Powell's projected film version of *The Tempest*, with James Mason and Mia Farrow.

R. M.

I

Shakespeare: from the Open Stage to the Screen

It is certainly difficult, and perhaps no longer possible, to free Shakespeare from the 'image' of the supreme poet and master playwright with which he has become encrusted during the past two centuries. The Shakespeare myth, with its principal shrine at Stratford-upon-Avon, began during the eighteenth century with Garrick's Shakespearean festivities at Stratford. The same period saw the foundation of genuine Shakespearean scholarship; Shakespeare and his works became the subject of continual study and research, but at the same time the victim of the pernicious idolaters, with their pursuit of bogus 'relics' and the exploitation of a new and thriving Shakespeare 'industry'.

Since that period the texts of the plays—turned into a form of holy writ—have been restored to what it is hoped may be their original form with a meticulous thoroughness which has become increasingly scientific. The conscienceless additions, deletions and interpolations made by the seventeenth- and eighteenth-century theatrical adapters were cut away—though the producers of the nineteenth century were not above adding their own touches to emphasize their mainly false ideas of the 'Bard' as a kind of romantic poet-prophet.

The combined effects of countless Shakespearean commentators, good and bad, and the commercial promotors bent on enticing the tourists and turning the 'shrine' into a permanent source of profit have made it almost impossible for us to sense the real man behind it all—the man who was once a working playwright living alternately in London and Stratford, producing scripts often, no doubt, hurriedly against time, helping to organize the company's succession of theatres in a sound and profitable way, paying respectful attention to the nobility and the Court, his primary patrons, and finally retiring to Stratford as a comparatively wealthy and much respected citizen, only to die in his early fifties.

His works have never been protected by such deterrents to interference as copyright. Their only real protection has been their own innate value and the increasing respect in which they came to be held. But their true value has often been disregarded or inadequately understood ever since Shakespeare's own century. Even when the text of the plays was restored to its rightful shape, the commentators and actor-managers were only too ready to misconstrue it. Because our 'objective' age seeks to discover all the facts, we have perhaps come closer to understanding Shakespeare than was the case in previous periods. At least we try to read his works in the context of the society and thought of his time as well as our own. Only the future can judge how objective in fact we have managed to be.

The twentieth century has experimented with the presentation of the plays in almost every conceivable form, including producing them in reproductions of the Shakespearean theatre itself. We have presented them in the round, on vast open stages, in the open air, in modern dress and even in the formalized style of Japanese Kabuki. They have been seen alike with expressionist, romanticist, cubist and social-realist sets, as well as in the celebrated combinations of space, light and movement devised by the great stage designer, Gordon Craig. Shakespeare himself could only have been staggered by it all had he been able to see what has happened to the plays he devised for the simple but effective stages of his time. And above all he would have been astonished to see his plays in the form of images on the cinema and television screens, the greatest transformation they have so far had to endure, but one which has brought their performance, often by actors and actresses who are among the best of our time, to audiences of millions across the world. What would he have thought of the fact that Laurence Olivier's film version of *Richard III* was seen on a single night's transmission coast-to-coast in the United States in 1955 by more people than had ever seen it in the theatres of England since the time it was first performed? The estimated audience was 62·5 million.

We shall discuss in this book the degree of artistic responsibility with which Shakespeare's plays have been transferred to the screen, primarily during the period of the sound film. Some four hundred Shakespearean films have been traced by Professor Ball during the silent-film period—few of them of any real significance because they could be little more than dumb show depending on the story-line of the plays, with occasional key lines mouthed to silent gesticulation. Among the more serious attempts to film Shakespeare's work in this frustrating silence were Johnston Forbes-Robertson's hour-long *Hamlet* (1913) and Emil Jannings's melodramatic *Othello* (1922). But only with the coming of sound could justice be done to Shakespeare's plays. Even so, there was a period, mainly during the 1930s, when the plays were to suffer in the hands of the film-makers the same kind of over-elaborate and romanticized treatment which they had received, for example, from Herbert Beerbohm Tree in the theatre at the turn of the century.

Let us for a moment consider Shakespeare's position as a professional writer in Elizabethan times, and compare it with the position of a writer for film or television today. Once he had achieved real status in his profession—that is early in the 1590s—Shakespeare probably adopted a fairly regular routine for his work. It would seem he divided his time between London and Stratford, which remained his home throughout his life, whereas London was the centre for his work. No doubt he wrote a substantial amount in both places; there is not only local evidence that he was frequently in Stratford, but also many indications of this in his work. His poetry is so immediately and continually responsive to nature, not only to the woodlands and the fields but to gardens and gardening. It is as if the moment he reached rural surroundings he could not help continually responding to them in his writing. He became, in fact, what we should term now a scriptwriter for a medium which, like the cinema and television today, required the services of a fluent dramatist who thoroughly understood his public and knew how to attract them to the particular theatre with which he was associated, working in competition with other, rival companies.

Shakespeare not only knew well how to write for his public; he knew how to write to please the members of his company, developing parts which could be expanded through their talent—such as the heavy characters of Macbeth, Othello or Lear, played by Richard Burbage, or the lightly imaginative parts played by Robert Armin, who could impersonate the Fool in *King Lear* with sensitivity or develop the volatile characters of Touchstone in *As You Like It* or Autolycus in *The Winter's Tale*. Shakespeare, himself an actor specializing in small but demanding roles, such as Adam in *As You Like It* or the Ghost of the King in *Hamlet*, doubtless had a firm hand in what would now be called the direction of the plays—though there is no evidence that the theatre of his time employed people actually as producers. We know that Shakespeare had strong views on acting —he put them into the mouth of Hamlet.

We know, too, that Shakespeare was a rapid and fluent writer from Ben Jonson's caustic remarks that he never appeared to revise or cut his work—as Jonson, a far more disciplined writer, certainly did. Jonson's is perhaps the best of all the contemporary comments on Shakespeare, which are so tantalizingly few and so elusive when it comes to giving any clear portrait of the writer about whom we want to know most. But Jonson is certainly quite specific; in *Discoveries* he brings us close to Shakespeare as a professional writer of the highest talent:

> I remember, the Players have often mentioned it as an honour to Shakespeare, that in his writing, (whatsoever he penn'd) hee never blotted out a line. My answer hath beene, would he had blotted a thousand. Which they thought a malevolent speech. I had not told posterity this, but for their ignorance, who choose that circumstance to commend their friend by, wherein he most faulted. And to justifie mine own candour, (for I lov'd the man, and doe honour his memory (on this side idolatry) as much as any.) Hee was (indeed) honest, and of an open and free nature; had an excellent Phantsie; brave notions, and gentle expressions; wherein hee flow'd with that facility, that sometime it was necessary he should be stop'd.

How like a profile of a modern scriptwriter this sounds—a writer whose work is in constant demand, with pressure to deliver yesterday rather than today. Jonson had a mind which was essentially critical, which means also self-critical. But his temperament was quite the opposite to that of Shakespeare; he was the Bernard Shaw of his

4

period, brilliant and cerebral. Shakespeare was the intuitive writer, unequalled when at the top of his form, pouring out alike verse which was power-driven in tragedy and exquisite in comedy, a writer deeply responsive to his prevailing mood, often writing badly (for a playwright of his outstanding quality) when time pressed him against his inclination, but with a superb resilience of imagination and verbal command when the mood to write was upon him. Though it is most unlikely he was lazy, he probably fell back into quiescent, recuperative moods after the exhausting process of writing such verse as the greater tragedies demanded of him. Perhaps he could not, at least for a while, look his writing in the face once it was done. This would annoy the meticulous Jonson. But writers who work fast and fluently often experience alienation from their work once it is set down on paper, and Shakespeare always had the period of rehearsal in which to make changes or to supplement his plays if this proved necessary—though rehearsal in the Elizabethan theatres was unlikely to have been as prolonged or as exacting as it is in the theatre today. The leading actors told the others what they wanted to do and where on the stage they wanted to do it—a tradition which stayed in the English theatre as late as the nineteenth century, even though Garrick and his successor, John Philip Kemble, paid considerable attention to the overall presentation and production of the plays.

The situation of the Elizabethan theatre, therefore, was in many respects remarkably parallel to that of contemporary film and television—closer in its own way than to the modern theatre. It inspired a great variety of plays, retaining in its permanent repertory only those which proved a draw, and dropping at once those which were failures. Its audiences were drawn from all classes of society with the money to pay for tickets—from the Court circle (with their 'command' performances for which they paid more or less adequately) to the common man. Everyone in those times, as today, felt he had the right to judge a play, and the discussions went the rounds about the latest play as they do today about the latest film. Dekker said as much in *The Gull's Hornbook* (1609):

> . . . the place is so free in entertainment, allowing a stoole as well to the Farmers sonne as to your Templer; . . . your Stinkard has the self-same liberty to be there in his Tobacco-Fumes, which your sweet Courtier hath: . . . and your Car-man

5

and Tinker claime as strong a voice in their suffrage, and sit to give judgement on the plaies Life and death, as well as the prowdest *Momus* among the tribe of *Critick*.

Dekker's ironic advice to the Gallants of the time instructed them on how best to steal the show by misbehaving during the performance. In fact, it was misbehaviour among the cosmopolitan audience just as much as fear of God which made the civic authorities so wary of plays, players and their audiences—as the wording of the Order of Common Council of 1574, just prior to Shakespeare's time, made only too clear in its reference to the plays which were put on in inn yards before the London theatres, modelled on these inn yards, were built:

> Whereas heartofore sondrye greate disorders and incon-
> venyences have been found to ensewe to this Cittie by the
> inordynate hauntynge of greate multitudes of people, speciallye
> youthe, to playes, enterludes and shewes. . . . Now therefore . . .
> by yt enacted that . . . from henceforth no Inkeeper, Tavern-
> keeper, nor other person whatsoever within the liberties of this
> Cittie shall openlye shewe, or playe, nor cause or suffer to be
> openlye shewed or played within the hous yarde or anie other
> place . . . anie playe, enterlude, comodye, tragidie, matter or
> shewe which shall not be firste perused, and allowed.

This was to lead not only to the licensing of theatres, but to the censorship of plays, which did not end in Britain until 1969. The succession of public theatres with which Shakespeare and his fellow players were associated were frequently regarded with as critical and hostile an eye as films and television can be today; far more so, in fact.

These general points about the Elizabethan public theatres are well known, and it was for these theatres that Shakespeare undertook by far the greater part of his work. His approach, therefore, had to be basically a popular one if his plays were to survive the patronage of so mixed a public as usually haunted the playhouses. But they were an intelligent, lively, open-mouthed public, speaking their minds, quick to sense a contemporary reference, enthusiastic about poetry, the expression of thought or passion, fascinated by the interplay of words in a language rapidly filling out its vocabulary, if not yet standardizing its spelling. The playhouses, like the taverns, were places where you expected to be kept in touch with contemporary events. Shakespeare's plays, therefore, like those of the rest of his fellow-dramatists, offered audiences a feast of sudden, half-concealed current comment, as critical as the writers dared in an age of arbitrary and authoritarian rule. The commentators of our period have discovered, as never before, the rich political significance not only of the long series of English historical plays but of the shorter series of Roman plays, which are among the greatest Shakespeare wrote— thirteen in all, over one-third of his total output of some thirty-seven plays in some twenty years of continuous work. The last thing that can be said of Shakespeare's plays is that they were remote from life, academic or 'classical' in the sense of being composed entirely under the influence of the past. Themes and events from the past were given contemporary significance, a point which certain directors of modern stage, film and television productions of Shakespeare have been quick to emphasize in a twentieth-century context—especially those responding to the influence of the Polish Shakespearean scholar, Jan Kott. All this makes Shakespeare's maturer work lively, edgy writing—fit not only for an actor to speak tellingly, but for an audience to receive with alert, responsive ears.

One of the greatest points of interest, therefore, in Shakespeare's maturer work is that, though the wording may from time to time be archaic or prolix after the better part of four centuries, the thought and the emotion behind it strike home with a modernity which often seems fantastic. Shakespeare wrote directly to, even *at*, his audiences, and when our common humanity is in question, as in all the great plays, what is said is as apt, profound and moving now as it must have been to the sensitive ears in his own time. Shakespeare's work has the perpetual astonishment of human revelation, enhanced by his uninhibited grasp of the language. The words spill out in a torrent, sometimes cascading over each other (to Ben Jonson's disgust) but, through the energy of his mind, constantly achieving a commanding truth of observation.

The rhetoric of bad Shakespearean acting from Shakespeare's own time to ours has dulled this quintessence of dramatic poetry. Today we try to find ways of speaking it which, while retaining the shape and rhythm of poetic utterance, do not lose the grasp of either thought or emotion in what is being said. The new media, with their emphatic close-shots, can be brought into full play to enhance and underline the significance of the words. Or they can, like the effusive stage productions of the nineteenth century, use spectacle and pictorialism to mute the sense of the lines, and turn Shakespeare's scintillating poetry into what sounds like the baying of human hounds.

Since Shakespeare's poetry is quickened by direct human experience we can only assume that, whatever happened between himself and his wife in the quiet backwaters of Stratford, he had known deeply both the pain and the ecstasy of love, perhaps many times over; that he knew also how to value the friendship of men; and that he was an exact observer of human behaviour in the social and political field. He was by nature a student of psychology; he understood the 'humours' (even today a not unreasonable approach to the divisions of human temperament) in so profound a way that modern audiences, given a clue to the psychological terms of the time (the phlegmatic, choleric, melancholic and sanguine temperaments), find it is themselves and their friends he is describing with the lucidity and sympathy of a wholly contemporary writer. The great range of Shakespeare's humane understanding, a product of the European Renaissance of which his writings are a part, has substantially helped to create the modern era. The Elizabethan and Jacobean age is the beginning of our own; it is not alien to our understanding as so much of the society of, for example, Chaucer's period appears alien to us— although Chaucer himself is Shakespeare's predecessor in bringing a humane mind to bear on the people of his time, who seem so very much more remote than those of Shakespeare's period two centuries later.

These, then, are among the considerations which contemporary producers of the plays in any form—stage, cinema, television— should have in mind when they attempt to bring out the values in Shakespeare's work through the medium they are using. The plays themselves, naturally, vary widely in their demands. Whereas *The Taming of the Shrew* can be taken more or less casually at surface value, *A Midsummer Night's Dream* may not, because it holds within its complex imagery and fantasy much that is not immediately apparent. This accounts for the radical difference between the film version of the play made by Reinhardt and Dieterle in 1934, which follows the more superficial, romantic interpretation of the nineteenth century, and the much-discussed, and frequently disliked, film made by Peter Hall in 1968, which owed something of its interpretation to the 'darker' view of the play as it is understood by Jan Kott. *Romeo and Juliet*, a beautiful stage poem belonging to Shakespeare's dramatic (and possibly personal) period of comparative 'innocence', functions as a play mainly on a single level of lyrical pictorialism, offset by the prose 'realism' of the character of the Nurse, which gives the play an added and earthy dimension. But there is not a great deal more than this to 'discover' through variant forms of emphasis in production, so that the three outstanding versions of the play in film—those of Cukor in 1936, Castellani in 1954 and Zeffirelli in 1968—all concentrate on the action and Italianate setting of the play, often at the expense of Shakespeare's poetic arias and recitative which, finely spoken, can be so affecting in a formalized stage presentation designed to give emphasis to the words.

But undoubtedly it is the profounder plays of Shakespeare's maturer experience which make the fullest demand on directors for both the stage and the screens, and these are the plays which have, for the most part, claimed the attention of the film-makers. There were, up to 1970, three sound versions of *Othello*, two of *Hamlet* (with a further notable version on British television, featuring Christopher Plummer), three versions of *Macbeth*, two of *Julius Caesar* (with a further notable amateur-produced feature, with Charlton Heston in early youth, in the United States), and two of *King Lear*.

The history of the adaptation of Shakespeare's plays for the screen is also the history of the adaptation of the screen to Shakespeare's plays. In fact, the principal fascination of this story is the various ways in which film-makers of distinction (notably Olivier, Peter Hall and Peter Brook of Britain, Orson Welles and Joseph Mankiewicz of the United States, Akira Kurosawa of Japan and Sergei Yutkevich and Grigori Kozintsev of the U.S.S.R.) have developed special techniques so that Shakespeare's dramatic structure and continuity, his characterization and his poetry will most effectively be served by the screen.

In this they are most fortunate, to begin with, in the form of stage for which Shakespeare had to work. This led him to construct his plays in a manner which closely resembles the structure of a screenplay. His action unfolds through a series of locations which were unlimited by any binding stage convention. Using no sets whatsoever, he could move as freely as he liked from place to place, indoors or outdoors—from house to street, from street to fields, from fields to cliffs, and from cliffs to the open sea itself. Even if, as in *A Midsummer Night's Dream*, a great part of the action takes place in a single location—the fairy-haunted forest—the characters move ceaselessly from one area in the location to another. The action always remains fluid.

Macbeth, to take one example, is only some two thousand lines in length; it is therefore one of Shakespeare's shortest plays, and about half the length of *Hamlet* in the fullest version. Yet it begins on a barren Scottish heath, moves to Duncan's camp, and then, after another scene on the heath, continues in Macbeth's castle at Inverness. The location then remains for some while in Macbeth's castle—but with scenes placed outside the gates, in an interior courtyard and in various rooms inside, those open to everyone in the castle and those private to Macbeth and Lady Macbeth. When Macbeth becomes King of Scotland the location moves with him to the Palace of Forres, while the murder of Banquo occurs on a lonely road near by. The banquet scene takes place in a room of state, and then the action moves rapidly between the heath, where the witches gather with Hecate, the cavern where Macbeth consults their oracles, various rooms within the Palace, and then the chamber in Macduff's castle where his lady and her son are killed. Not content with staying in Scotland, Shakespeare takes us south to the King of England's palace. The final action alternates between various parts of Dunsinane Castle and the woods near by, from which the rebel armies advance beneath the cover of branches hacked from the trees. In the imagination of Shakespeare and his co-operative audience, the action shifts the location twenty-five times. Or, to take another great play of far larger dramatic proportions and even looser geographical structure— *Antony and Cleopatra*. This moves spectacularly through forty-two changes of scene, covering places as various as Alexandria, Rome, Messina, Misenum, Syria, Athens and Actium, and including simulated battle actions on both land and sea. The parallel with the cinema is obvious.

In fact, Shakespeare's theatre used only a few stage properties and occasional signs to indicate a change of place to the eye. There are, of course, many fine descriptions, usually at the beginning of scenes, to start the visual imagination as to the place and atmosphere of the scene. But Shakespeare was free in time and space—a form of freedom impossible in any kind of modern realistic, or even semi-realistic picture stage, using scenery which is even remotely representational. The habit has grown up to present the plays—as often at the theatre in Stratford-upon-Avon—against the single, unified background of some large-scale, imagistic structure representing the prevailing atmosphere of the play as the producer understands it. But Shakespeare's original intention was the very opposite of such static sets— he wanted his plays to drive forward without any intermission in one continuous flow of movement from place to place—often indicating with words thrown in here or there the nature of the setting, where this mattered to the atmosphere of the moment. The film today, possessing real scenic mobility, can let the audience actually see the places to which the action moves, and through the arts of design, lighting and photography can give these places an appropriate dramatic atmosphere. The structure is the same as in Shakespeare, but the method of presentation filled out with fully realized backgrounds or locations.

In his handling of his sources, such as Holinshed or Plutarch, Shakespeare, like any screenwriter of today, was ready to make free with history, or what purported to be history, if he believed a firmer dramatic line would be the result. The critics of the time complained that Shakespeare's contemporaries, or near-contemporaries, distorted the facts, as critics have often complained in our time about films dealing with historical characters. Writing in 1580, the critic using the strange name of Anglo-phile Eutheo complained of the Elizabethan dramatists of the period:

> —if they write of histories that are knowen, as the Life of Pompeie; the martial affaires of Caesar, and other worthies, they give them a new face, and turne them out like counterfeits to showe themselves on the stage. It was therefore aptlie applied to him, who likened the writers of our daies with Tailors, who having sheers in their hand can alter the facion of anie thing with another forme; and with a new face make that seeme new which is old.

Here, indeed, in the Elizabethan theatre, was a new, popular and, in many respects, uninhibited form of entertainment, as the cinema was to become in the twentieth century. In order to exist at all, it had continually to attract considerable audiences. The unruly genius of Marlowe gave it power and vitality; Shakespeare inherited his splendid melodrama and 'mighty line', and he eventually acquired a cast of players who were to form the star combination of talent in the English theatre of the later 1590s and the early years of the seventeenth century. Almost all Shakespeare's plays were written for the public as distinct from the private theatres of the period, and in the absence of any law of copyright, were, as everyone knows, drawn from every available source—older plays, chronicles, biographies and popular romances, many of Italian origin.

On the same principle that a film producer buys the film rights of popular novels, plays or biographies today, Shakespeare was constantly on the watch for subjects he could adapt which suited his own taste and that of his company and their audiences. He was often prepared to mingle the good material with the merely conventional, throwing in his hand as if he had grown suddenly weary of the whole business. His plays, like our own contemporary films, used, and sometimes exploited, violence of action and language; he introduced the contrived 'happy end' with marriages which often seem as forced as they are unsuitable, marriage being used as a kind of sovereign remedy for past ills, as at the close of *All's Well that Ends Well*, which is otherwise a sharp and even profound play, one of his series of dark 'comedies'. He introduced low comedy, obscenity and even slapstick. The plays also exploited pageantry, processions, masque-like interludes and colourful displays of every kind popular with audiences of the time. All these things are there for their box-office value, and we tend to tolerate them in Shakespeare, whether well or badly done, because of the unequalled value of the best in his work. He knew the popular appeal of glamour and romance, of costume and music, of violence and even sadism, as in the notorious *Titus Andronicus*. The cruder taste of the Elizabethan audience was in many essentials the same as the cruder taste of cinema audiences today, and there has scarcely been a period since the plays were written when they did not hold some fascination for the public. Today their capacity to draw audiences on many levels is still unique, and through film and television these world-wide audiences have been fantastically enlarged from hundreds of thousands to tens or even hundreds of millions.

It is therefore of the greatest importance that the techniques of presentation adopted by the new media should not stop short at exploiting the single, most obvious aspect of Shakespeare's adaptability to the screen—the fluidity and excitement of the action. It is evident that Shakespeare's profoundest values lie in the dialogue, the dramatic poetry and prose with which he clothes and humanizes the action. This would appear to be obvious, but one remembers the vandalism to which his works were subjected until Garrick and his successor, John Philip Kemble, in the eighteenth century restored some semblance of respect for the dialogue as Shakespeare wrote it and as the responsible commentators of the period had begun to evaluate it. But, like the actor-managers of the nineteenth century, many of those who present Shakespeare in our own time on the stage are prepared to use their blue pencils with too great a freedom and insensitivity, making drastic cuts, if not actually re-writing the text of the plays to suit the purpose of their particular productions. It is scarcely to be wondered at, therefore, that the film-makers, faced with the necessity of adapting the plays to a different, some would say an alien, medium, are tempted to make free with the text, cutting it back to the barest essentials in order that they may carry the action forward in broadly pictorial terms.

However, we must distinguish between the English-language films and those, like the Russian and Japanese, which use a translation. In the principal Soviet films, the text used is Pasternak's translation, which is written in slightly heightened prose, a sensitive and direct approximation of Shakespeare's poetry, but, of course, with the lowered intensity of prose. In the case of Kurosawa's *The Throne of Blood* (the title in Japanese, *Kumonosu-Djo*, is *The Castle of the Spider's Web*) the text is by Kurosawa himself, though he dispenses as far as possible with dialogue, creating an astonishing atmosphere by special qualities of setting, acting, sound effects and music. Yutkevitch, Kozintsev and Kurosawa are at pains to transmute Shakespeare's poetic-dramatic atmosphere into visual terms—not merely reproducing the action with appropriate sections of dialogue, but carefully replacing Shakespeare's poetic imagery with imagery re-conceived visually. This is specially true of Kozintsev. In the case of the English-language films, which have used, very naturally, Shakespeare's densely written, complex speech composed over three and a half centuries ago, everything must be done to make what is visual direct the attention of the audience to the values or implications of what is being said by the actors. It is for this reason that certain modifications of normal film technique have come to be adopted, as we shall see.

It is well known that the degree of almost hypnotic attention we pay to what we *see* (especially in the artificial conditions of the darkened cinema with its highly lit screen) is very much greater than the attention we give to what we *hear*. (Anyone who has tried to avoid reading the subtitles in a foreign language he knows, when the film is in fact being spoken in his own language, is most forcibly reminded of this.) Listening to prolonged periods of speech (such as a radio talk, a lecture or a play) requires special concentration, which we give willingly only if our interest is fully aroused, as it is in the theatre. Films, however, depend as an art to a large extent on what is presented for observation by the audience—using this act of observation as subtly as the poet uses his verbal imagery and rhythms to captivate the ear. Speech in film comes as a part of this act of observation, much as it is used in real life; we *observe* people talking, often paying at least as much attention to their facial reactions, gestures or bodily behaviour as we do to their actual choice of words. We take in their total *manner of expression*. This is the point at which the director of a film using Shakespeare's actual text has to make a decision concerning how exactly he will captivate the attention of the audience so that they will be induced to concentrate on the fuller significance of what is being said. And to a certain extent he is once more helped by the techniques Shakespeare had to adopt in making full use of the large stage in the Elizabethan public theatres.

This stage extended out into the auditorium, so that the actor could walk at will to the forestage, and literally be among his audience. Shakespeare, himself an experienced actor in these theatres, wrote on what might be termed a sliding scale according to the degree of intimacy, or otherwise, with which the actor was to treat his surrounding audience. The 'aside' was obviously spoken directly to them, as if sharing a confidence. The soliloquy, or spoken thought, was a sharing of the more intimate reactions of the character with the audience, which the actor could treat either as a direct address to them (as Gloucester in *Richard III*, Edmund in *King Lear* and Iago in *Othello* obviously do) or as something wholly private to the character which they are privileged to overhear, but which is not specifically addressed to them as a conscious act of communication by the character. Speeches conceived on the larger scale—such as those spoken by Henry V to his soldiers, or Antony to the Roman crowds in *Julius Caesar*—were oratory which dominated the whole theatre, supporting player and audience alike. Dialogue, the principal area of Shakespeare's dramatic writing, was obviously composed to be spoken by the characters face to face, person to person, with no conscious playing to the audience at the same time—at least by the kind of actors Hamlet (speaking for Shakespeare) wanted to see working in the theatre. This scaling of Shakespeare's dramatic writing for a theatre which permitted so varied a relationship between actor and audience according to what part of the stage area he was using, also lends itself to the varied scale of performance required in a film, according to whether the actor is being shown in long shot or close shot. Soliloquies in films can be actually presented as spoken thought—as in both Laurence Olivier's and Grigori Kozintsev's film versions of *Hamlet*— the words spoken, but by unmoving lips. Or they can be addressed to the audience from the screen as a sharing of confidence—as in Olivier's *Richard III*. In the film, the mob oratory of Antony in *Julius Caesar* need no longer be addressed to a few extras backed by the 'crowd' formed by the audience themselves. Large crowds can, of course, be assembled on the great sets built for a film, and a new dimension of production, undreamed of by Shakespeare, achieved through the far greater physical resources of the cinema.

These various adventitious aids increase the effectiveness of Shakespeare's words. But there can be little doubt that the full-scale spoken poetry of Shakespeare's stage and the continuous visual imagery of the cinema can be oil and water. It is the business of the director of a Shakespearean film to make them as compatible as possible by imaginative compromises in production techniques. Judicious, as distinct from wholesale, cutting is one compromise. But the visual 'pointing' of the speeches—with careful scaling of their delivery in close shot in order to elucidate meaning by thoughtful, not oratorical, means—is the best way, avoiding the intrusion of distracting reaction shots, but supporting the poetry by any legitimate means available, either visual or aural, including the use of musical phrasing. So the Chorus's speech in *Henry V* describing the preparation of the French army for attack is supported by off-screen sound effects and coloured by musical phrasing, while Laurence Olivier's delivery of the soliloquy, 'To be or not to be', is supported by the sound and, occasionally, the sight of the wash of the waves on the rocks below, or the shot of Hamlet's dagger which drops from his nervous grasp into the sea.

But the most powerful of all images on the screen is the human face itself. If the actor speaks his lines with a fine judgment both for their meaning and for their poetry, the fact that we are watching from so close a position can only serve to reinforce what is being said. The only compromise, therefore, is the need always to use the medium with restraint, avoiding any unnecessary or distracting visual effects. Film-makers must accept this particular discipline if they are to be effective in presenting Shakespeare from the screen—whether in the cinema or on television. The degree of success achieved by those distinguished film-makers who have tried their hand at adapting Shakespeare for film or, in certain cases, television, will be discussed and illustrated, together with the principles in technique which they have collectively evolved through trial and error in the past.

However, it can be claimed that Shakespeare's dramatic art is best fulfilled on the screen through an uncompromising transmutation of everything for which his words stand into an entirely new form, made up of images-with-sound. In this case much, or even at times all, of what he wrote for a stage where everything had to be created in the imagination of the audience through the speech he put into the mouths of his actors, may well have to suffer a 'sea-change into something rich and strange'—poetry cast in the mould of another medium as potentially powerful in its own right as his own. This explains the extraordinary rightness of Kurosawa's totally transformed version of *Macbeth, The Castle of the Spider's Web* (*Throne of Blood*), in which virtually nothing of the original text remains in recognizable translation. It would indeed be an odd outcome to our discussion if it transpired that Shakespeare's plays stand the best chance of a wholly satisfying transfer to the screen in those countries which are farthest removed from his overwhelming verbal influence.

2

Shakespeare and the Silent Film

Some four hundred films adapted from Shakespeare's plays have been traced during the period of the silent film.[1] Shakespeare's plays offered a rich source for plots, especially during the early years when film producers were turning to literary and theatrical sources in order, as they hoped, to raise the standard of films and lift them out of the fairgrounds into respectable entertainment. The movements in France and Italy known as the *film d'art* and *film d'arte* inevitably sponsored the filming of Shakespeare, often in the form of absurd little charades lasting five or ten minutes, high-lighting the key scenes from the better-known plays. Some of the earliest of these films afford glimpses of eminent actors and actresses miming scenes from Shakespearean characters they had made famous on the stage.

The first Shakespearean film of all was a brief record made in 1899 of Sir Herbert Beerbohm Tree as King John signing the Magna Carta, filmed on the London Embankment. This scene does not occur in Shakespeare's play, and is therefore a harbinger of many other 'inspired' additions to the plays which were to appear in films to come. Other early curiosities include the duel scene from *Hamlet* with Sarah Bernhardt as the Prince (1900), a film with sound recorded on wax cylinders for phonograph accompaniment, a blue-tinted film version of the storm and shipwreck from Beerbohm Tree's production of *The Tempest*, and a ten-minute version of *Hamlet* by Georges Méliès (1907) in which he appeared as the Prince. Méliès usually created fantasies, but he also made a film of *Shakespeare*

Writing Julius Caesar (1907). Billy Bitzer, D. W. Griffith's celebrated cameraman, produced the duel scene from *Hamlet* in the United States in 1905, and Griffith himself made *The Taming of the Shrew* in 1908. According to Professor Ball, 1908 became a vintage year for Shakespeare, initiating a whole series of one-reel productions—some fifty in all—which were to continue to be produced until 1911, made principally by the Vitagraph and Thanhouser companies in the United States. The plays adapted in this truncated form included *Macbeth, Richard III, Othello, Romeo and Juliet, King Lear, Antony and Cleopatra, Julius Caesar* and *A Midsummer Night's Dream*; Vitagraph's principal directors were William V. Ranous, a very capable Shakespearean actor of the old school, and Charles Kent, an actor of some distinction who had lost his voice and therefore liked working in silent films. Edwin Thanhouser, another actor from the American stock companies, made a two-reel version of *Romeo and Juliet* in 1911; later, as the length of feature films increased, longer versions appeared from Vitagraph and Thanhouser, mainly of the comedies—for example, a two-reel *The Merchant of Venice* and a three-reel *As You Like It* (1912), a two-reel *Cymbeline* (1913) and a four-reel *The Merchant of Venice* (1914). A spectacular five-reel *Richard III*, costing £30,000, featuring Frederick Warde, was produced in 1913. A curiosity of Shakespearean film history is Theda Bara playing Juliet in *Romeo and Juliet* (1916).

The *film d'art* movement promoted Shakespeare in both France and Italy. Paul Mounet (brother of the better-known actor, Mounet-Sully) appeared in a one-reel version of *Macbeth* (1909–10); Italy produced the inevitable *Romeo and Juliet* as well as *Hamlet* in 1908, and a *Julius Caesar, Othello* and *Macbeth* in 1909. Mounet-Sully recorded at least the graveyard scene from *Hamlet*, and there were other versions of the play made in France before the better-known Danish version of 1910, which was shot at Kronborg Castle at Helsingör (Elsinore) directed by August Blom, who is reputed to have shot some 12,000 feet of film in the few days during which the castle was placed at his disposal, though the final film was released at only some 1,200 feet. Hamlet was played by the German actor Alwin Neuss. The most prominent of Italy's Shakespearean productions of this period, *Brutus* (1910), made by Italy's senior director, Enrico

Guazzoni, in a single reel, was praised at the time for the cinematic treatment of the key action scenes. Other Italian films included two versions of *King Lear*, another *Romeo and Juliet* and a *Merchant of Venice*. Guazzoni was in 1914 to present a four-reel *Julius Caesar* of outstanding quality, though only very partially based on Shakespeare's play. The great French actor, Harry Baur, appeared as a comic Shylock in a two-reel version of *The Merchant of Venice*, called, rather incongruously, *Shylock, ou le More de Venise* (1913). Among the oddities of this period was *The Real Thing at Last* (1914), a burlesque version of *Macbeth*, scripted and initially directed by James Barrie, and produced by A. E. Matthews. The all-star cast included Edmund Gwenn, Nelson Keyes (as Lady Macbeth), Godfrey Tearle and Leslie Henson, while the witches appear to have included Gladys Cooper, Fay Compton and Pauline Chase.

The British film-makers were not idle. The celebrated Will Barker shot *Hamlet* in a single day at his studio in Ealing in 1910 with Charles Raymond as the Prince, and the following year paid Beerbohm Tree £1,000 for the privilege of filming his spectacular stage production of *Henry VIII*, in which Tree played Wolsey, Arthur Bourchier the King, Violet Vanbrugh Katherine, and Henry Ainley Buckingham. Tree, however, was apparently not anxious for his work to be placed on permanent record, and insisted in his contract on the prints of the film being destroyed after their period of exhibition. Sir Frank Benson, on the other hand, allowed an interesting if somewhat ludicrous version of his production of *Richard III* in 1911 at Stratford-upon-Avon to be recorded, and it survives as a series of melodramatic tableaux of key scenes from the play. Previous to this, his productions of *Julius Caesar*, *Macbeth* and *The Taming of the Shrew* had all been filmed in 1911. Mrs Basil Rathbone, who appeared in *Richard III*, told me that the company took a week to make the film at Stratford, working in the mornings prior to appearing on the stage in their normal repertoire. Benson's acting, with its exaggerated gesticulation, seems at times wildly over-theatrical, but he believed in strongly marked, rhetorical performances derived from his long training with Sir Henry Irving.

Another distinguished actor who had been trained by Irving was Sir Johnston Forbes-Robertson, and the film he made with Cecil Hepworth of his final production of *Hamlet* before his retirement in

1913 is among the few good and genuinely revealing Shakespearean films to survive from the silent period. The cost of this six-reel, feature-length production was put at £10,000; it played one hour and forty minutes, and it was accompanied by a special music score adapted from Tchaikovsky. Directed for Hepworth by the actor E. Hay Plumb, the film used elaborate locations in addition to sets built in Hepworth's studio at Walton-on-Thames, and modelled on the stage sets of Hawes Craven, once Irving's stage designer. A reconstruction of Elsinore Castle was erected at Lulworth Cove, and some locations were shot in the grounds of Hartsbourne Manor in Hertfordshire, the home of Maxine Elliott, Forbes-Robertson's sister-in-law. The production, if somewhat over-tied to the theatre in certain interior scenes, is acted with innate dignity and restraint, and Forbes-Robertson's performance as Hamlet, with its beautiful movement and rhythm of gesture, anticipates the scale of acting needed for such close observation by the camera.

During the war, production declined in Britain; only a single *Merchant of Venice* appeared in 1916, an undistinguished production featuring Matheson Lang as Shylock and his wife, Hutin Britton, as Portia.

In 1916 Beerbohm Tree was signed at a reputed fee of £100,000 to work on a series of films with D. W. Griffith as producer and John Emerson as director, the first to be *Macbeth*, with Constance Collier as Lady Macbeth. Although the film was successful with the critics, it failed with the public; a dispute with Tree followed, in which attempts were made to cancel the contract. This did not deter Metro from releasing another *Romeo and Juliet* in the same year, featuring Francis X. Bushman and Beverley Bayne, or Thanhouser from producing *King Lear*, featuring Frederick B. Wade. Italy produced another *Hamlet* in 1917, starring Ruggero Ruggeri and directed by Eleuterio Rodolfi; those reels which survive are considered by Professor Ball to be the most cinematic yet produced from a Shakespearean play, though still over-theatrical in treatment and acting.

After the war, the film industries of Europe began to re-establish themselves, giving increased attention to the production of feature films. The films of the 1920s in both Europe and the United States became star vehicles of ever increasing elaboration and cost, and outgrew the wide-scale and over-obvious pilfering of stories from

Shakespeare or any other classical source. Audiences wanted both spectacle and at least the semblance of sophistication. However, a few films of some note were made which derived their themes directly or indirectly from Shakespeare—the first being the Danish actress Asta Nielsen's German film, *Hamlet* (1920).

One of the earliest stars to understand the nature of film acting, Asta Nielsen concentrated her intense performances upon small and revealing details of behaviour. Her film, which was directed by Svend Gade and Heinz Schall, did not derive from Shakespeare but from a special adaptation of the Hamlet story derived by Edward P. Vining from Saxo Grammaticus (Shakespeare's source, along with another Elizabethan play on the subject); in this version of the story Asta Nielsen played Hamlet as a woman disguised as a man. She is therefore a Princess, not a Prince, in love with Horatio, and filled with a woman's scruples about killing her stepfather. This striking, if implausible, adaptation of the Hamlet story is by far the most interesting film of the 1920s to have any link with Shakespeare's work, since the two other adaptations, both German—*Othello* (1922),[2] with Emil Jannings as a brutal Othello, and Werner Krauss as Iago, and *The Merchant of Venice* (1923), also with Werner Krauss (who was, of course, celebrated as the impersonator of Dr Caligari) as Shylock and Henny Porten as Portia—were both relatively undistinguished as films. *The Merchant of Venice* also played free with both the story and the names of the characters—Portia is changed to Beatrice and Shylock to Mordecai. Germany also produced an unorthodox version of *A Midsummer Night's Dream* (1925), directed by Hans Neumann, which had to be 'forbidden for juveniles' owing to the lascivious behaviour of Valeska Gert as Puck and the general Rabelaisian nature of the comedy. Werner Krauss appeared again—this time as Bottom the Weaver.

There was little of Shakespeare in either the British or American films of the 1920s, though several took hints from Shakespeare and incorporated them into plots which had no direct link with his works. For example, Buster Keaton believes he is playing Hamlet momentarily in his film *Day Dreams* (1922). By the middle 1920s filmmakers realized that only a few years stood between them and the sound film. It was better to wait until Shakespeare could be filmed with speech.

1. Professor Robert Hamilton Ball's thoroughly researched book *Shakespeare on Silent Film* is the principal source for this chapter. See also Ian Johnson, 'Merely Players' (*Films and Filming*, April 1964); *Shakespeare Film* (Deutsches Institut für Filmkunde, 1964). A number of the more important Shakespearean adaptations are preserved by the National Film Archive, including Sir Frank Benson's *Richard III* (1911), Sir Johnston Forbes-Robertson's *Hamlet* (1913) and *The Merchant of Venice* with Werner Krauss (1923).

2. In his book *Réflexion Faite* (1951), René Clair wrote of this film with more generous praise than others have done: 'Forget *Othello*, forget Shakespeare's text. Don't be afraid; all that's necessary is for you to recall the spirit of the play. Go to see the film as you would attend a concert; here is a symphony of images inspired by Shakespeare's theme. Certain expressions on the faces of Othello and Iago correspond literally to the text. Elsewhere, the presentation of the shots, their continuity, the inner movement of the film recall Shakespeare in a manner worthy of him. This film is no banal parasite of a great work. . . . One can readily accept that the director, imbued with the spirit of the play, put the book aside and thought only of the images it evoked. This is the only proper way to adapt. Emil Jannings is an Othello . . . black, thick-lipped, heavily sensual . . . a stupid child, urged on by Iago. . . . Buchowetzki . . . is not afraid to offer us an Iago who is almost a clown . . . Iago's soliloquies, his treacherous words . . . are conveyed on the screen by movement.' (pp. 54–5.) The director was Dmitri Buchowetzki.

3

The Arrival of Sound: The First Phase of Adaptation

No time was lost. With the establishment of the optical track in the cinemas during 1928–9, Shakespeare's dialogue was at last to be heard, though from the most unlikely source. Mary Pickford and Douglas Fairbanks produced *The Taming of the Shrew* in 1929, appearing as Katharina and Petruchio under the late Sam Taylor's direction; the film appeared in both a silent and a sound version, which was not uncommon during the uneasy period when only a proportion of cinemas were equipped with sound. The sound version of this film became notorious for its initial credit: 'Written by William Shakespeare with additional dialogue by Sam Taylor.' The purists were shocked, and the film immediately discounted.

The play is, in many respects, an unpleasant one to modern taste, since it involves the humiliation of a high-spirited woman who has developed into a termagant. The process of 'taming' her no doubt made the Elizabethans laugh, and the convention of laughing at such a situation has survived with the play merely because it is by Shakespeare and stays in the popular range of his work on the stage. It provides plenty of opportunities for farcical action, and is usually played with a kind of rough good humour which allows Katharina to score a few points over her braggadocio husband. Though the play, an early one written probably during 1593–4, is relatively short, the text is not normally treated with much respect in the theatre; the spoken word is often severely cut, while the stage business between Katharina and Petruchio is stretched out to win more laughs.

This is precisely what Sam Taylor's production did; the struggle was developed into a farcical battle between Douglas Fairbanks and Mary Pickford.[1] When he destroys the marriage bed by flinging mattress and coverlets on the floor, she takes her place there demurely as if it were the most comfortable place imaginable; when his back is turned, she flings a stool at his head. She only feigns agreement with his extravagant demands, and delivers the final speech on wifely obedience with a wink to the other women. Given that the play has to be cut and adapted in order to be made presentable to popular audiences, and taken rather more tongue-in-cheek than (possibly) the Elizabethans understood it, *The Taming of the Shrew* was not a negligible film in terms of unsophisticated screen comedy. But it merely used what was left of the text as a string of words spoken with high spirits to accompany the action. In spite of its stars, however, it was not successful.

I am grateful to my friend Laurence Irving, Douglas Fairbanks's and Sam Taylor's designer for *The Taming of the Shrew*, for additional details about this production. Laurence Irving had originally gone to Hollywood in 1928 to work on Douglas Fairbanks's production of *The Man in the Iron Mask*; he assisted the designer, William Cameron Menzies, later to be the director of Korda's production of *Things to Come* in Britain. *The Man in the Iron Mask* was directed by Sam Taylor, who is described by Laurence Irving as 'an endearing, gangling collegiate New Yorker who had won his golden spurs directing Harold Lloyd's comedies and Mary Pickford's teenage romances'. He claims that the Fairbankses were attracted to make a film of the play because of their early stage experience; virtually the whole of Hollywood saw the coming of sound as an invitation to film plays with artists who had had stage experience. Douglas Fairbanks was proud of his stage background, and used to delight in giving Laurence Irving imitations of his celebrated grandfather, Sir Henry Irving. Nevertheless, the studio was dubious about Shakespeare's powers at the box-office, and Laurence Irving heard one film salesman remark to another: 'Sure, we're making *The Taming of the Shrew*, but we're turning it into a cah-medy.' He writes:

> Indeed, Sam Taylor was doing so with unsophisticated zeal. Day and night he was attended by two gagmen—rude non-sensicals after the Bard's own heart—with faces like battered

bantam-weights and an inexhaustible fund of practical comicalities in the Mack Sennett tradition. Whenever dialogue that could not be cut tended to lag or was reckoned incomprehensible to the ninepennies, they were called upon for a diversion. And here and there Sam, who was a secret dramatist, interpolated a line or two in the vernacular. Constance Collier joined us as English-speaking governess to the production, thus reinforcing Mrs Eleanor Glyn, who for some time past had been the mentor of silent Hollywood on the modes and manners of English polite society.

Laurence Irving did his best to persuade Sam Taylor not to make himself a laughing-stock by insisting on his credit for 'additional dialogue', but in vain. 'Well, I did the stuff, didn't I?' was all Sam Taylor would say in reply. Douglas Fairbanks undertook the part with a shadow on his heart; he hated the sight of the padded cell which the embryonic sound studio had become. 'Laurence,' he said, 'the romance of film-making ends here.' His voice proved, in Laurence Irving's view, 'too thin to match his robust action', but Mary Pickford's Katharina he found 'engagingly shrewish'.

There were to be no more Shakespearean films until 1934, when Max Reinhardt's celebrated stage conception of *A Midsummer Night's Dream* was produced as a film by the Warner Brothers, jointly directed by Reinhardt and William Dieterle. For Dieterle, who had emigrated in 1930 to the United States from Germany, where he had been distinguished both as actor and director, *A Midsummer Night's Dream* was to be his first film of distinction in Hollywood; in a note written for the author he says of Reinhardt:

> This remains one of my most pleasing professional memories, largely because I had, of course, been his devoted admirer ever since I had been fortunate enough to play under his direction in the Deutsche Theater as a young actor in my twenties. The *Dream*, of course, had been one of his favourite productions for decades, and I had had considerable experience of it. Contractually, we were given equal credit (he, of course, being named first), and it was clearly understood between us that he was to be concerned with dialogue and leading the actors, while I attended to all technicalities connected with the filming. Inevitably there was some overlapping but everything went without a hitch and in the most pleasant atmosphere, simply because we understood each other so very well.

25

The film cost $1½ million, ran for over two hours, and failed at the box-office. Nevertheless, it was by far the most spectacular attempt of the decade to present Shakespeare on the screen, rivalled only by M.G.M.'s highly pictorialized version of *Romeo and Juliet* which was to follow hard upon it.

Reinhardt's spectacular stage productions, centred on Berlin but well known elsewhere, had been a feature of the European theatre since the period preceding the First World War. Among his larger-scale presentations was *A Midsummer Night's Dream*, in which he developed the fairy element in the play along romantic, magical lines until it dwarfed the rest with its lighting effects and choreography; he took this production, with others, to the United States in 1927–8. With the rise of Hitler he left Germany. He presented *A Midsummer Night's Dream* for the Oxford University Dramatic Society at night in a beautifully lit open-air production; later he was to produce the play again in Hollywood itself. As a result of this, Jack L. Warner ventured into setting up Reinhardt's production as a film, insuring himself at the box-office by introducing as many stars as he could into the cast—whether they were appropriate or inappropriate. They included James Cagney (Bottom), Joe E. Brown (Flute), Mickey Rooney (aged 11, Puck), Anita Louise (Titania), Victor Jory (Oberon), Dick Powell (Lysander), and Olivia de Havilland (Hermia). The choreography for the fairies was devised by Bronislava Nijinska and by Nini Theilade, who played the principal fairy. Among the team of directors of photography was Byron Haskin, head of the Special Effects department at Warner Brothers, and some twenty years later to be closely associated with George Pal in the production of outstanding science fiction films.

The choreography and special effects, in fact, make the principal value of the film, as a film. The whole nineteenth-century romantic concept of the production arises from Mendelssohn's score which, arranged by Erich Wolfgang Korngold, pervades the atmosphere; there is even a miniature orchestra of dwarfs present in the wood to assist in the performance. If one accepts Mendelssohn's interpretation of the fairy wood (as distinct from the far darker concept of Shakespeare's intentions, as understood by Jan Kott, for example, or represented in Peter Hall's stage and film productions of the play a generation later), then the commanding performance of Victor Jory as Oberon amply fulfils Reinhardt's intentions, while Mickey Rooney's urchin Puck stands somewhat left of centre—not sinister enough for Kott, not elfin enough for Mendelssohn.

An even further disparate element came with the lovers—Dick Powell, in particular, introduced a light-weight presence which, admirable in its place, could bring little which could be relevant to this Mendelssohn-Shakespearean film. Again, the hard professional clowning of Joe E. Brown established an alien atmosphere in the third element of the play, the rustics, while James Cagney, with his own form of tough sophistication, made Bully Bottom into a relatively straight character which was once more out of sympathy with the rustics as a whole. The text of the play was cut back by over half, and its order sometimes changed in the interests of visual continuity. With a running time of 140 minutes, it is the choreographic spectacle of the corps de ballet of the fairies to which Reinhardt constantly returns, with such startling effects as the absorption of the fairy train at dawn into Oberon's long, magic cloak. However much one may object to the characterization, to the truncated lines, to the speaking, or non-speaking, of Shakespeare's verse, much of the film is still strangely effective in its own particular right. Even so exacting a critic as John Russell Taylor [2] does not mind admitting this:

> Not, clearly, a 'serious' approach to Shakespeare at all, and yet, strange to relate, a remarkably successful film, one which even today is fresh and vivid when its more worthy, respectable contemporaries look hopelessly faded. However dubious it may all look on paper, in the cinema it nearly all works. The performances, if sometimes a trifle odd, are lively and interesting, and Mickey Rooney's Puck is absolutely brilliant. The fairy sequences in particular, shot through spangled gauze for the most part, distil precisely the slightly cruel, slightly sinister poetry that Shakespeare achieved in words, often by cutting the words and replacing them with visual equivalents of startling beauty. Oddly enough, Reinhardt the stage director has in his only film managed to do what most experienced film directors have hardly considered doing: he has translated Shakespeare instead of merely recording him.

Two other Shakespeare films were to be released in the same

period—*Romeo and Juliet* (1936) directed by George Cukor and produced by Irving G. Thalberg for M.G.M., and Paul Czinner's Anglo-American production of *As You Like It* (1935-6), made in Britain with a budget of $1 million. *Romeo and Juliet*, with Norma Shearer (aged thirty-five) and Leslie Howard (aged forty-two), cast as the adolescent lovers in order to ensure some returns at the box-office, was given the full M.G.M. treatment of the period; its sets, designed by Cedric Gibbons, were great decorative structures in studio-Italianate style—the luxurious Capulet ballroom, the great central square of Verona, where the street fighting takes place, the formal moonlit garden at the end of which stands the high circular balcony of Juliet's bedroom, the bedroom itself (gay at first, sombre when Juliet drinks her potion), the tomb full of sarcophagi where Romeo searches frantically for her. An area of one hundred acres was set aside to build the sets for Verona; Cedric Gibbons created fifty-four basic models, and the design for sets and costumes, and even for some of the action, was derived from the works of Gozzoli, Botticelli, Carpaccio, Fra Angelico and Bellini. For example, the procession of the Prince of Verona was based on Gozzoli's *Procession of the Magi.*

A good example of the transmutation of description in the play into action in the film is the pestilence story in Act V, Scene ii:

FRIAR LAURENCE: This same should be the voice of Friar John.
   Welcome from Mantua: What says Romeo?
   Or, if his mind be writ, give me his letter.

FRIAR JOHN: Going to find a barefoot brother out,
   One of our order, to associate me,
   Here in this city, visiting the sick,
   And finding him, the searchers of the town,
   Suspecting that we both were in a house,
   Where the infectious pestilence did reign,
   Sealed up the doors, and would not let us forth,
   So that my speed to Mantua there was stayed.

FRIAR LAURENCE: Who bare my letter then to Romeo?

FRIAR JOHN: I could not send it, here it is again—
   Nor get a messenger to bring it thee,
   So fearful were they of infection.

FRIAR LAURENCE: Unhappy fortune! By my brotherhood,
  The letter was not nice, but full of charge
  Of dear import; and the neglecting it
  May do much danger. Friar John, go hence,
  Get me an iron crow and bring it straight
  Unto my cell.

FRIAR JOHN: Brother I'll go and bring it thee. [Exit.

FRIAR LAURENCE: Now must I to the monument alone;
  Within this three hours will fair Juliet wake.
  She will beshrew me much that Romeo
  Hath had no notice of these accidents.
  But I will write again to Mantua,
  And keep her at my cell till Romeo come—
  Poor living corse closed in a dead man's tomb.

In the published screenplay of the film, this becomes:

232 VILLAGE OF PLAGUE—AFTERNOON—INT. HOUSE OF
  PLAGUE—FRIAR JOHN in doorway, now open, looking back into
  the room. The pallet is empty, fumigating torches are burning.
  FRIAR JOHN goes out into street.

233 STREET OF PLAGUE—IN MIST—OVER MUSIC. We see a
  death cart with body, as the grave-diggers take it away, preceded
  by an 'Apparitore'—a bailiff of the meanest kind, whose office it
  is to warn passers-by, by the sound of a little bell, to retire.

  In background we see a dense column of murky smoke from a fire
  in which clothes, beds and other articles of infected furniture are
  burning. Passers-by flee at the approach of the death cart. Other
  villagers are praying at a wayside cross.

  As FRIAR JOHN comes into street, soldiers enter scene with his
  horse. He mounts and rides off hastily toward Verona. [Cut to:

234 VERONA—FRIAR LAURENCE'S CELL—EVENING—FRIAR
  LAURENCE. Vesper bells are ringing. FRIAR LAURENCE is
  looking at hour-glass.

235 CLOSEUP HOUR-GLASS. The sands running through slowly
  but steadily as we—   [Dissolve to:

236 ROAD BETWEEN MANTUA AND VERONA—NIGHT—
  ROMEO AND BALTHASAR. Camera travels with ROMEO as he

rides through the night, his face set, his eyes straight ahead, oblivious of night, road and man.

Under the DISSOLVE that precedes this scene we go from vesper bells to the slow, measured beat of the distant curfew bell in Verona, which continues through scene.   [Dissolve to:

237   FRIAR LAURENCE'S CELL—NIGHT—
FRIAR LAURENCE AND FRIAR JOHN
FRIAR LAURENCE is greatly agitated.

FRIAR LAURENCE: Who bare my letter then to Romeo?

FRIAR JOHN: I could not send it—[*Gives it to* FRIAR LAURENCE.] Nor get a messenger to bring it thee, so fearful were they of infection.

FRIAR LAURENCE: Unhappy fortune, by my brotherhood, that letter—the neglecting of it may do much danger! [*Takes a lantern.*] Now must I to the monument alone. [*Looks at hour-glass.*] Within this three hours will fair Juliet wake. She will beshrew me much that Romeo hath had no notice of these accidents; but I will write again to Mantua, and keep her at my cell till Romeo come. [*Turns away.*] Poor living corse, closed in a dead man's tomb!
                                        As he hurries away we FADE OUT.

The speaking of the verse by Norma Shearer and Leslie Howard was never less than professional. As Ellen Terry once said, citing an old tradition in the theatre: 'An actress cannot play Juliet until she is too old to look like Juliet.' The truth of this is made evident by the various Juliets we have seen on the screen: neither Susan Shentall, in the version of 1954 by Castellani, nor Olivia Hussey in Zeffirelli's film of 1968 knew how to compass the verse—both, however, looked splendidly in character. Norma Shearer, a fully mature actress, gave the lines all the intelligence and feeling her years commanded, but she appeared utterly out of character, a middle-aged woman masquerading as an adolescent virgin. Leslie Howard, though over forty, did his best to bring a youthful ardour and sincerity to the poetry, but his evident age made his task impossible.

Finally, there was Paul Czinner's million-dollar *As You Like It*, a film which made little mark, even though Laurence Olivier appeared as Orlando. The production was once again a victim of the star system. Paul Czinner's wife, Elisabeth Bergner, whatever her merits as an actress in modern plays and films, had a screen personality diametrically opposed to that of Rosalind. Rosalind is a forthright woman, capable, provocative and determined beneath her surface diffidence and charm. Elisabeth Bergner's screen character was exactly the opposite—she derived her charm from depicting an age-less, kittenish quality in women, a kind of self-destructive femininity, half innocent, half knowing, which inevitably led to frustrated in-fatuations with a tragic outcome. She had the habit of turning somer-saults, and did so as Rosalind. Nevertheless, the film brought to-gether a notable creative team; Carl Mayer helped with the script, Lazare Meerson (René Clair's designer from France) was responsible for the décor, the choreography was by Ninette de Valois, while William Walton wrote the first of his scores for Shakespearean films; the cast included Henry Ainley as the Duke and Leon Quartermaine as Jaques. But the film was inevitably centred upon Elisabeth Bergner's Rosalind, with her anxiously inappropriate characteriza-tion and the velvety coo of her foreign accent. However, though one critic complained of her 'temperamental inability to stop wriggling', another referred to her as 'an imp of delicate enchantment'.

J. C. Trewin, the drama critic, wrote in *Sight and Sound* after seeing *As You Like It* on the screen: 'What do I remember? Elisabeth Bergner as the archest, most infuriating kind of Rosalind-Pan. A flock of sheep. Another flock of sheep. The voice of Henry Ainley. Laurence Olivier's Orlando stopped at every turn by this coy and romping Rosalind.' Another reviewer, John Marks, writing in *Sight and Sound*, referred to 'this wanton and worldly Rosalind'. However, he conceded that 'Leon Quartermaine's delivery of the Seven Ages of Man speech was magnificent. He and Olivier found themselves in a talkie, and made the most of it, when they strode backchatting through Arden. But what an Arden! Fake flora and genuine fauna prodded in from the wings.' He preferred *Romeo and Juliet*, and makes the following interesting comment for its date (Autumn 1936) [4]:

> Personally we still don't see why they have to film Shake-speare, except that he was the first man to write scenarios—good scenarios, too—cuts, continuity, comp. shots and all. But if they must, it is something that his successful translation into active cinematic terms should have started—at last—with a certain dawning realisation that it's the dialogue that counts, however difficult verse may be to film, and that, though it is

rich in metaphor and so is the screen, because its pictures dance, allude and illustrate, yet the camera is not always obliged to skip as quick as thought; so that not invariably when the poet mentions, say, a bear, need we have one lumbering into view.

In Thalberg's production (directed by Cukor) Shakespeare is appreciated as a librettist: the camera serves to clarify the incidents and outline of his plot. That is half the battle—the easier half. His words are poetry, an awkward fact which most of Thalberg's actors did their best to overlook, shying as far as possible into prose.

Basil Rathbone, a versatile, capable actor, was the exception; his Tybalt was excellent. But to film Shakespeare, with all the magnificent resources of the screen at one's disposal, to use them well—though much too lavishly—and yet to miss, or dodge, the verbal values of his poetry, is surely to fail, without excuse, in an enterprise which deserved to be undertaken with greater confidence. As we feared, the Midas touch of Metro-Goldwyn-Mayer has frozen (and perhaps thwarted) the designs of Mr Oliver Messel.

Lush or finicky, and sometimes lovely, the film's construction of Verona is as uneven as it is varied. The stage is evidently set for some solemnity; love's tragic pyre is marvellously contrived; all that is lacking is the fire of passion.

More interesting still is the little-known intervention of Bernard Shaw into the debate. On 23rd October 1936 Shaw took part in a debate on the speaking of Shakespeare in the film when introducing a lecturer on screen diction, Dr Esdaile, in the M.G.M. private theatre in London. Shaw was, of course, a recognized authority on diction, and was deeply attracted by the potentialities of the sound film. Among the remarks he made at this session for the film industry, as reported in *World Film News* (November 1936) were the following:

> Too often in the talkies we have a cast made up of people who all speak very much at the same pitch and in the same way. If you want to get a really effective performance you ought to be very careful to make your voices vary. When I cast a play I not only bear in mind that I want to have such-and-such a person for one part and such-and-such a personality for another part, but I want to have a soprano, an alto, a tenor and a bass. A conversation on the stage in which they all speak with the same trick and at the same speed is an extremely disagreeable thing and finally very tiring. You have to select your voices

so that they will contrast and you have to bear in mind that your microphone will bring a number of little nuances and changes which, as I say, would be quite impossible on the stage.

We have not thought enough about these things. In spite of the popularity of the film, nobody to whom you talk ever talks about the voices or about wanting better voices, or understands anything about phonetics. . . . The contrast of voices will make a film very pleasant. . . .

Q. Is it possible to do justice to Shakespeare's verse as verse through the medium of the screen?

G.B.S. I should go so far as to say that you can do things with the microphone that you cannot do on the ordinary stage. I want again to emphasise the fact that you are dealing with a new instrument and that in speaking on the screen you can employ nuances and delicacies of expression which would be no use spoken by an actor on the ordinary stage in the ordinary way. They might possibly reach the first row of the stalls; they would not get any further. . . .

The main thing that you require nowadays is to get people who understand what they are saying when they are speaking Shakespeare. That is really the difficulty, because you must remember that Shakespeare's language is to a great extent a dead language. . . . .

And I may say that I think the difficulty of avoiding monotony is largely a question of people understanding what they are saying.

You see if people do understand and feel what they are saying they get all sorts of inflexions without thinking about it. Of course if they are only repeating lines they have picked up, not only is the thing monotonous, but it is unintelligible, because they never fix the key-word and get it across. You always have to look out for the one word without which the speech is unintelligible.

Q. With the use of the camera you are able to get the spirit of the aside, the soliloquy, much better than you are able to get it on the stage. . . ?

G.B.S. That is very interesting. Because one of the difficulties now is to keep the camera in its place. Often in a studio I have seen an enthusiastic photographer wasting any amount of money and time in order to get a certain little spot of light over the door, which did not matter in the slightest degree, and at the same time a number of actors were having to repeat themselves over and over again until they became lunatics almost. But there it is. It is a very admirable illustration of what can be done. Really the whole business of the screen is a most wonderful art. Nobody I think has yet had the least idea of how much can be done with it. In fact we are at present in the stage when anybody who really knows what can be done with it gets cast out of the studio because he knows nothing about it!

Q. Don't all these devices in themselves constitute an interruption of the verse, the rhythm, the sweep of the verse?

G.B.S. Well, if they are not used in the proper way, of course they not only spoil the verse but they spoil everything else. It is extraordinary how much can be spoiled if you let the photographer, as photographer pure and simple, get the upper hand. There is the human voice; you have the verse and the lines. They may be deliberately distorted for some reason, but you have to be careful. You have to remember for instance that you are speaking Shakespeare, not giving an exhibition of photography. . . .

With the actor in such stuff as, say, the big scenes of Shakespeare it is not a matter of voice altogether. He must be continually looking out for the moment when he can get down to nothing in order that he may have some room to get up again. It is part of the trick of Shakespearean acting, that you give the illusion that you are a sort of human volcano, going from one summit to another. These special tricks have got to be learnt for the screen as well as for the theatre. . . .

One thing I have to warn you about. In good drama I don't think we are going to lose altogether what we call the Shakespearean effect. If anybody imagines that the dialogue in my plays is natural, they are making a fearful mistake. I write exactly like Shakespeare and I find if only people will get the rhythm and melody of my speeches, I do not trouble myself as to whether they understand them, so to speak; once they get the rise and fall of them they are all right.

The common characteristic of these four adaptations from Shakespeare during the 1930s is that none of them displayed any realization that an imaginative adaptation of normal film technique would be necessary to allow Shakespeare's greatness as a dramatist to reach its proper fulfilment through the screen. The mid 1930s was possibly the wrong period for this to be understood or attempted; film-

34

makers were still over-preoccupied with establishing the first principles of matching sight and sound, while at the same time rebuilding an impregnable star system after the silent era in order to sustain the very costly medium which the sound films had become. Producers attracted by the powerful appeal of Shakespeare's name and the superficial filmic quality of his plots and settings also knew what they were risking in putting his work—with the lengthiness and archaism of the dialogue, the subtleties of his poetry, the complex appeal of his characters belonging very much to a past culture as well as to 'all time'—before the greater public of the cinemas, with their taste for the obvious in drama and their predilection for star personalities. Although one need not for a moment doubt the good intentions of the producers of *A Midsummer Night's Dream, Romeo and Juliet* and *As You Like It*, they inevitably leaned for safety's sake in the direction of 'processing' the plays in such a way that the public would never lose sight of the fact that these films, like all other 'prestige' productions, were primarily vehicles for performances by favourite stars and for costly pictorial presentation.

Shakespeare's dramatic intention, indeed the very nature of the plays, was obscured and finally all but lost in the need to give first place to the film industry's idea of 'production value'.

Nevertheless, there was a great deal to be learned from these initial attempts at filming Shakespeare, and the first person to profit by them was Laurence Olivier, who had not at first thought that Shakespeare could be filmed satisfactorily. Eight years after his experience as a player in *As You Like It*, he was to undertake his first assignment as a film director with *Henry V*. He came to film-making as a keen Shakespearean. He was as conscious of the need to make the film serve Shakespeare as he was of the need to make a good film out of Shakespeare's play. With his films of *Henry V, Hamlet* and *Richard III* we were to see the first imaginative adaptations of the plays to the screen.

Notes to Chapter 3

1. According to Mary Pickford the film was made at the period when the rift in the Fairbanks marriage was becoming apparent. See her autobiography, *Sunshine and Shadow*, 1956, pp. 311–12.

2. In *Shakespeare: a Celebration*, edited by T. J. B. Spencer, pp. 109–10.

3. Leslie Howard was the third choice for the part, which had been offered first to Clark Gable (aged thirty-four) and, secondly, to Laurence Olivier (aged twenty-eight). The latter refused it on the grounds that 'Shakespeare could not be filmed'.

4. See also the amusingly acid debate for and against *Romeo and Juliet* between C. A. Lejeune and Val Gielgud in *World Film News*, December 1936.

4

Laurence Olivier and the Filming of Shakespeare

Laurence Olivier's associations with Shakespeare on the screen go back, as we have seen, to his appearance as Orlando in Paul Czinner's *As You Like It* (1936). He was then under thirty, and had made his reputation as a Shakespearean actor on the stage the previous year in *Romeo and Juliet*, alternating Romeo and Mercutio with John Gielgud.

HENRY V (1944)

Henry V was the first of Laurence Olivier's essays into the filming of Shakespeare. *Henry V* was a play suitable for the national situation of Britain at war, poised to invade German-occupied France. Agincourt, it is true, was scarcely a suitable parallel to the D-day landings, but in any case the film was not finished in time to coincide with this historic day, its timing kept secret by security. But to produce, direct and play the title role of *Henry V* was a great task, even for so well-established a film and stage actor as Olivier had become. In addition to playing Orlando, which at least enabled him to gain direct experience of speaking Shakespeare before the camera, he had seen the initial attempts by Dieterle and Cukor to make the plays effective on the screen. He set out to do it quite differently. Talking to me in 1955, just after the completion of the filming of *Richard III*, Laurence Olivier said:

> . . . The film climax is a close-up; the Shakespearean climax is a fine gesture and a loud voice. I remember going to George

Cukor's *Romeo and Juliet*. As a film director he did what seemed the right thing when he took the potion scene with Norma Shearer—he crept right up to a huge head, the ordinary film climax. But it was in fact a mistake. She, being a good technician in film-making, cut the power of her acting down as the camera approached her for the climax of the speech leading up to taking the potion—'Romeo, I come! This do I drink to thee.' At the moment of climax she was acting very smally, because the camera was near. That was not the way it should have been. So the very first test I made for *Henry V* I tried to see how it would work in reverse. It was in the scene with the French Ambassador, and as I raised my voice the camera went back —the exact opposite technique to that in *Romeo and Juliet*— and I have done that ever since. There are moments when you want to be in the front row of the stalls seeing every line of the actor's face, and there are moments when you say 'I wish I was in the back of the gallery for this scene'. These are the only moments when you use the top shot, or so it should be. I think there is much less difference between film acting and stage acting than people think—much less. If you are a long way off in the dress circle you are really no further away than in a long shot. The exception, perhaps, is the big head—the ordinary close-shot is rarely much closer than the front row of the stalls. Your acting should be just as careful on the stage as it is on the screen, because there are always people who can see it. . . .

Henry V was to be a great prestige success when it was finally released in 1944. Its warmth and virility, as well as its nationalistic emotionalism, suited the buoyant mood of wartime Britain after the successes in Europe, and its rich colours and rousing music stirred the imagination in the grey days of a Britain still living with ration-books, utility clothes and houses needing paint.

The text, prepared during 1943 with the help of the critic Alan Dent, was cut back by about one-third, and the scene of Falstaff's death from *Henry IV*, Part II was added.[1] A major decision in presentation was to open the film with a slow crane-shot over a vast model of Shakespeare's London, with the camera coming to final rest on the Globe Theatre, where a performance of *Henry V* is about to start. This introduction, establishing time and place, is backed by William Walton's descriptive music. The actors bustle about in the green room as the audience assembles in the pit and the galleries, while some sit on stools on either side of the apron-stage. Then, after the trumpet-blast announcing the start of the performance is blown from the turret of the theatre, the play begins with the Prologue splendidly spoken by Leslie Banks, setting the scene and period of the play. The play itself begins with the somewhat tedious dialogue between the bishops; only when the action involving King Henry himself is fully established does the frame-structure of the performance in the Elizabethan theatre give place to the direct action of the film. The Elizabethan audience is forgotten.

This second phase introduces a new type of setting. From the comparative realism of the reconstructed Elizabethan theatre, the play moves into settings which derive from pictures approximating to the historical period of Henry V, the backgrounds and costumes shown in such detail in the mediaeval illustrations for the *Calendar of the Book of Hours* of the Duke of Berry, executed by the brothers Limbourg, or the illuminations in Froissart's *Chronicles*. Many of the sets directly reproduce the shallow, stylized perspective of these paintings and miniatures, bringing their own striking theatric quality to the environments in which the action is played, the characters appearing like figures moving in a three-dimensional painting. The film was photographed in Technicolor by Robert Krasker in order to enhance this entirely pictorial, anti-realistic atmosphere. The courtship of Henry and Katharine of France, for example, became a decorative, animated miniature, though to those who normally prefer a realistic approach in film the combination of real people with settings in which the human figures are normally portrayed in as stylized a manner as their backgrounds, proved at times incompatible.

The battle of Agincourt, which was added by Olivier to the action of the play, had by its nature to be carried out on location, and this added a third phase to the design of the film. The initial inspiration for the battle scenes came in part from the battle on the ice in Eisenstein's film *Alexander Nevsky* (1938), with its long lines of horsemen ranged along the distant skyline waiting the command to charge; another source was the massed grouping of horsemen in combat in Uccello's *Rout of San Romano*. The location was set up in neitral Eire; members of the Eireann Home Guard appeared as the French and English knights and soldiers. The battle scenes and their prelude, occupying rather less than ten minutes in the film, took some thirty-nine days to film, and a rail-track a mile long was laid down so that the camera mounted on a vehicle might be driven alongside the charging lines of the French cavalry.[2]

After Agincourt, the film returned to its mediaeval settings, and finally to its frame inside the Elizabethan theatre before the final captions rolled up the screen to the heroic theme of Walton's concluding music. The score is possibly the best, the most inventive he devised for Olivier's Shakespearean films.[3] The music for the Agincourt sequence rose to a climax, merging the orchestra with the whirr of the English arrows and the clangour and cries of battle. Other sequences which stay in the memory are the death of Falstaff with Mistress Quickly's homely lamentation, the speech of the common soldier on war spoken simply and sincerely in a West-country accent, the Chorus's speech descriptive of the armies preparing overnight for battle (pointed by Walton's subtly descriptive music), and the deeply emotional scene of the King himself, disguised and isolated, wandering through the camp at night and meditating on the responsibilities of the monarch in time of war. The camera becomes identified with the King, moving through the camp of sleeping soldiers, while Olivier's tense, thoughtful voice speaks Shakespeare's incomparable lines.

HAMLET (1948)

In 1946 the opportunity came to film *Hamlet*, with a budget of some £475,000. Although he had played Hamlet at the Old Vic in 1937, Olivier was at first unwilling to play the part in the film, as distinct from directing. In *The Film Hamlet*, he wrote: 'I feel that my style of acting is more suited to stronger character roles, such as Hotspur and Henry V, rather than to the lyrical, poetical role of Hamlet.' Leaving aside the somewhat romantic concept of Hamlet's character that this statement represents, it is interesting to note that Olivier has been quoted as saying of Henry V that 'the difficulty in Henry's character is its complete straightforwardness'. Nevertheless, in the end he was forced to play Hamlet in the film, and with a characteristic gesture he dyed his hair blond 'so as to avoid the possibility of Hamlet later being identified with me'. The film was to win five Oscars and receive an award at the Venice Film Festival.

The film treatment of *Hamlet* is very different from that of *Henry V*.

The action takes place in a vast but unified structure—a series of sets, large and small, which combine to establish the effect of a castle-prison, barren of all but the most essential furniture, and decorated only by formalized murals. Huge columns give some of the larger interior shots the appearance of a cathedral nave. Some of the exteriors, notably the ramparts where Hamlet meets the Ghost, are platforms with neutral, blacked-out backgrounds or areas of mist, lit only by pools of light directed from above. The actors often become figures shown in silhouette. A recurrent feature is the vistas seen at the end of long, empty corridors, or the view through a sequence of rooms linked by successive archways. At one moment Ophelia is framed by an archway in the distance, and then Hamlet is seen at a similar distance in reverse. The grouping of actors in the longer scenes leads to constant patterns reminiscent of Eisenstein's later films—the figures in the foreground framing or offsetting those in the background; this is strikingly done, for example, when the Ghost is framed by the static silhouettes of the observers on the ramparts. The effect of all this pictorialization is intentionally artificial, indeed highly theatrical, and is in contrast to the comparatively naturalistic appearance of occasional outdoor scenes—for example, the ramparts above the sea where Hamlet soliloquizes, or the graveyard where Yorick's skull is discovered, or the rather out-of-place, Millais-like scene of Ophelia's body floating in a real stream on the studio lot.

The black-and-white photographic treatment of *Hamlet* has been criticized for the over-use of travelling shots, the camera tracking, panning and circling around the sets and the actors. Hamlet is seen for the first time sitting apart in the Court when a movement by Laertes is followed through with the travelling camera until the whole Court group is included in the frame; this is completed when the Queen, and later the King, move over to Hamlet's side to create a new grouping in the manner of the theatre. The close of the film, when Hamlet's body is being carried to lie in state in the tower on the ramparts, brings a prolonged survey of the whole castle, place after place exciting association with earlier scenes in the film. Crane shots, moving high up or low down, emphasize the nature of the action; for example, the camera glides from the roof of the great hall down to the seated figure of Hamlet, deep in thought preparatory to the first soliloquy, only cutting to a big close-shot at the words 'solid flesh' in the initial line. The camera lifts high up above the actors three successive times in order to emphasize the conspiratorial plotting of Hamlet's death by Claudius and Laertes. In general, the individual shots are held for a longer time than normal in films, and quick cutting is rare—though it occurs notably during the Ghost scene ('′Tis here! ′Tis here! ′Tis gone').

This emphatic visual treatment is reinforced by verbal effects. Hamlet's distracted visit to Ophelia is presented in mute mime as Ophelia's voice describes his appearance and actions. Later, Ophelia's body floats in the stream while the Queen is describing the circumstances of her death, and Hamlet's adventures at sea (as he later relates them to Horatio) are seen performed in mime. Most striking of all, the play scene before the King is presented as a mime set to music, the camera circling, now to one side, now the other, behind the throne-chairs where Claudius and Gertrude sit, with close-shots showing their cumulative reactions to the mime; finally, when Claudius rises with the cry, 'Give me some light!', it is Hamlet who thrusts the torch into his hand when the Court disperses in turmoil. The music in the play starts in an archaic style, vaguely suggestive of period, and then develops gradually into a fuller form of orchestration.

Those of Hamlet's soliloquies which are retained [4] are treated as a mixture of voiced thought and direct speech. For example, the speech, 'O! that this too too solid flesh would melt', begins with Hamlet's expressions responding to the significance of the words which are heard spoken on the sound track as he wanders thoughtfully in the empty hall, finally going up to the King's throne-chair and leaning on it; only with the words, '—and yet, within a month—' do his lips move in direct speech. In the later soliloquy, 'To be or not to be', music and the natural sounds of the sea provide a backing to the spoken thought—direct speech only coming suddenly into play with the words, 'perchance to dream'.

Laurence Olivier introduces certain impressionistic effects, most strikingly in Hamlet's encounter with his father's ghost. The shock is shown directly—the image pulsates in and out of focus to the thud of Hamlet's heart-beats.[5] The Ghost itself is not seen at first; we only get these powerful reactions to its presence, with many close-shots revealing the details of Hamlet's response to the awesome spectacle of his dead father. The camera lifts momentarily skywards, then back to mid-shot, Hamlet reacting as much by gesture as by word, though his repetition of the Ghost's first allusion to the 'murder' is uttered with a kind of wondering horror. A montage of shots follows, showing him climbing through mist in the wake of the moving Ghost. When the Ghost is finally seen in close-shot, it is faceless—a kind of bearded skull. The Ghost's description of his murder by Claudius is accompanied by its re-enactment in gauze-masked mime, like a dream presented in a slow dissolve. At the end of it all, Hamlet collapses, and is seen lying on a large circular rostrum from which the camera cranes up to a height, looking down on his prone figure.

The acting is full of detailed touches, similar to those of Hamlet's reaction, throughout. The light-haired wig used by the boy-player in the travelling company suddenly reminds Hamlet of Ophelia's blonde hair; the scene with Yorick's skull becomes peculiarly moving because the skull, seen in close-shot, becomes like a real person—an effect all but impossible to achieve on the stage. Ophelia's child-like behaviour with Laertes, obviously a much-admired elder brother, reveals early on her extreme youth, and her utter incapacity to act with independent judgment when she is exploited later on by her elders in their conspiracy against Hamlet. In contrast to these often delicate points of detail is the bravura of performance so dear to Laurence Olivier, revealing him to be a theatrical showman as well as a great artist. The duel scene, lasting ten minutes and taking fourteen days to shoot, is magnificently intense, with the growing rage of the contestants. The melodramatic flying leap down from a height onto Claudius, when Hamlet plunges his sword into his uncle's body at the end of the play, is in tune with similar effects practised in the theatre—for example, in the production of *Coriolanus* at Stratford-upon-Avon in 1959; Olivier was at one stage hung upside down, grasped by the ankles. The jump was sufficiently dangerous to be made the final shot in the production.

William Walton's music, as in *Henry V*, brings its own rich colouring to the atmosphere of the production—though it is used rather more sparingly than in the previous film. Its developed use in the play scene has already been noted. There are musical themes associated with the characters, notably with Ophelia and with Hamlet himself. The Hamlet theme is first used at the opening of the film; at the end it is fully developed as Hamlet moves in tempo with it down the flight of stairs to the area where the duel is to take place, and again when his body is carried up to lie in state on the ramparts. Throughout the film, music is constantly used as a bridge to cover changes of mood between scene and scene, or incidentally, to cover such bridging actions as court processions and the like.

Of the three Shakespearean films directed by Laurence Olivier, *Hamlet* is possibly the one which most repays detailed examination. It may have certain marked faults, and even *longueurs*—camera movement is sometimes inexplicably overdone, becoming technically selfconscious and destroying the atmosphere. Moments of pictorialism can strike a false note—the Millais-like shot of Ophelia's body in the stream has already been mentioned. The film, though over-long, suffers from certain important losses through the drastic cutting of the text. But this *Hamlet* remains nevertheless arguably the most imaginative of the three films in treatment and realization, as it is, obviously, by far the most demanding of the three as a play. It was decided at the outset deliberately to restrict its scope, and at once to define and delimit its theme by the emphatic recitation, by Laurence Olivier himself, of the lines spoken by Hamlet to Horatio which are offered as the key to Hamlet's character:

> So oft it chances in particular men
> That through some vicious mole of nature in them,
> By the o'ergrowth of some complexion
> Oft breaking down the pales and forts of reason,
> Or by some habit grown too much; that these men—
> Carrying, I say, the stamp of one defect,
> Their virtues else—be they as pure as grace,
> Shall in the general censure take corruption
> From that particular fault.

As Olivier himself says at the beginning of the film: 'This is the tragedy of a man who could not make up his mind.' And it is on this level that the character is portrayed without any further sophistication beyond, perhaps, a somewhat enigmatic relationship between Hamlet and his mother who, as played by Eileen Herlie, appears rather to be Hamlet's sister than a woman a generation older.

44

Writing of the sets, the designer Roger Furze said in *Hamlet: The Film and the Play*:

> Almost all of the action was to happen in the castle at Elsinore. Olivier wanted a dream-like, cavernous place as the setting for a drama which is centred in shadowy regions of the hero's mind. . . . Most of the arches are Norman; the wall paintings are suggestive of the Byzantine; the tapestries are in the style of a rather later period. The castle is there as a setting for action, not as a demonstration of styles of architecture. . . .
>
> This business of levels is particularly suited to the cinema, and the action of *Hamlet* continually invites it. The topmost tower of the battlements, for instance, might almost be given a credit title among the actors. It is the first thing to be seen when the film opens, and it reinforces the dramatic effect on several occasions. It is to this lonely height that Hamlet is led by the Ghost, and the supernatural dread of the moment is intended to be increased by a sense of physical danger. . . . From the same dizzy height Olivier speaks the celebrated 'To be or not to be', which is a meditation on suicide. The means of suicide are very close at hand. Finally, they bear Hamlet's body to this topmost tower when the tragedy is over.

The film was shot in black and white, not colour. Olivier himself has said in *The Film Hamlet*:[6]

> Colour had been essential for *Henry V*. In *Hamlet*, I did at one time examine the notion of filming it in subdued colour—blacks, greys and sepias. But on further consideration, I felt that the final effect would not really have justified the extra problems which use of the Technicolor camera always involves. When we came back to our decision to use black and white, it had the added immediate advantage, that it could be combined with deep focus photography, whereas we could not have done this had we used colour.
>
> Apart from the obvious advantage, for a film in verse, that deep focus photography enabled us to shoot unusually long scenes, it had the extra merit of lending itself to shots of extreme beauty. I have in mind in particular one shot nicknamed 'The longest distance love-scene on record'. . . . In some cases, an actor is over 150 feet away from the camera. . . .

The initial conception of the film, Olivier has said, grew from a visualization of the final shot.

Again, the film is bound together by the music of Walton. For example, Muir Mathieson writes in *The Film Hamlet* of certain sections of the score, including that for the play scene:

> The arrival of the Court is heralded by trumpet calls and a superb march theme which appears to keep step with the retinue as they take their places around the King's dais. Then the players make their entry, accompanied by a small group of musicians. For this, Walton hints at the idiom of the period, and uses an orchestra of two violas, cello, oboe, cor anglais, bassoon and harpsichord. He opens with a sarabande, music in slow three-in-a-measure dance time often encountered in 17th and 18th century music, and follows this with a slower, sinister passage for the entry of the poisoner.
>
> As the camera moves round to show the reactions of the audience, and particularly of the King, the stage music dissolves into the Players theme, which is taken up by the full symphony orchestra, as the dramatic undercurrent of the scene, and the tension of the Court, rises. The camera, from its circular track-orbit, returns to the Players, and the music reverts to the quiet accompaniment of the play. The actor-king has been poisoned; the King can no longer stand the strain. ('The play's the thing, Wherein to catch the conscience of the King.') The full power of the orchestra rises up, swamping the soft sounds of the cello, oboe and harpsichord, and ends in a tremendous chord, as the King roars out, 'Give me some light'.

I am grateful to Laurence Olivier for the following information about the setting up of *Henry V* and *Hamlet* by Filippo Del Giudice, the Italian producer who became managing director of Two Cities Films, and was responsible for such productions as *In Which We Serve*, *Brief Encounter*, *The Way Ahead* and *Odd Man Out*, as well as *Henry V* and, initially, *Hamlet*. Laurence Olivier writes:

> I think Del heard me doing the 'breach' speech on the radio when I was in uniform, and I met him first, I remember, on the opening night of *In Which We Serve* (1942). I found his attitude in the matter of the obtaining of my services somewhat over-confidently expressed, as a lot of people did on first encounter. However fond one got of him, and I got to be extremely fond indeed, one was never quite able to feel tolerant towards his boastfulness, and I think it was this element in him that to some quite large degree brought about his downfall. As in so many thousands of instances people put up with

46

eccentricities of character so long as the owner of that character is successful, but not in other circumstances, though once I'd started working with him his blazingly flattering convictions of one's worth as an artist were irresistible.

I was to learn that he had an almost heroic side to him. During the eight weeks I was in Ireland to get ten minutes on the screen for the battle in *Henry V*, a few rain-sodden rushes would eventually find themselves in his projection room in Denham, which resulted in nothing but praise and encouragement, while at the time (I was to learn later) he was undergoing quite a bit of persecution from the many backers and under constant threat from them, none of which Del gave me the slightest inkling of.

The film cost £475,000, and this after a budget by me of no more than £300,000. Conditions, you must understand, were very far from favourable. We had only one Technicolor camera in the country, no quick cranking gear box, equipment at Denham so incomplete that an entirely new and costly lamp-hanging job had to be done if one wished to turn the camera from one to the opposite direction. Days and days of precious time were wasted owing to this and other disadvantages naturally imposed by wartime conditions.

Del did succeed in setting up *Hamlet*. This having been achieved, he disappeared from the picture, having settled to part from Rank and Two Cities, and set up his own new company called Pilgrim Pictures. In fact, I remember having great difficulty in getting his name onto the credits.

Del Giudice had formed a financial and distribution link with J. Arthur Rank over a period of years, and this had enabled him to set up *Hamlet*. After a short period in the United States, Del Giudice retired to Italy in 1952, and eventually entered a Benedictine monastery. He died in 1961. The revival of quality films in Britain during and immediately after the war owed much to his flair, and without him Laurence Olivier's first two Shakespearean films would probably never have been made.

RICHARD III (1955)

Then came the offer from Alexander Korda for a film version of *Richard III*. It was a formidable play to adapt. Concerning cutting back Shakespearean plays, either for stage performance or film, Laurence Olivier has said, 'the same basic problems remain, of reducing the length, elucidating the plot, unravelling irrelevancies, and relating the result to the type of audience'. Talking to me in 1955, after the formidable task of filming *Richard III* (once again with the expert help of Alan Dent), Olivier said:

If you are going to cut a Shakespeare play, there is only one thing to do—lift out scenes. If you cut the lines down merely to keep all the characters in, you end up with a mass of short ends. This is one of the problems with *Richard III*. To start with it's a very long play. It's not until the little Princes come on that the story forms that nice river sweep, going swiftly to its conclusion from about half way through the play. The first part up until that moment is an absolute delta of plot and pre-supposed foreknowledge of events. After all *Richard III* forms the last part of a cycle of four plays, the other three being parts of *Henry VI*.

Alex Korda asked me to do it, and both Vivien and Carol Reed helped persuade me to tackle it. I had hoped that Carol Reed would direct it, but it was not possible. Nevertheless he made a lot of helpful suggestions. But he would keep on saying, 'Larry, we must have a scene written between King Edward IV and Jane Shore!'

It's a really difficult play to film—it's involved, often obscure. Yet it's always been a popular play—as Dr Johnson said, its popularity derives from the character of Richard. But I felt it absolutely necessary to do more simplification than I've ever done before, and although every commentator and critic through the centuries had attacked the structure of this play, I quite expect, now, to be accused of vandalism. And yet some of the most famous lines like 'Richard's himself again' and 'Off with his head, so much for Buckingham' are not Shakespeare's at all, but were added later by Garrick or Cibber, who thought nothing of adding scenes adapted from *Henry V* to their productions! The film runs two-and-three-quarter hours, and of course ends with the battle scenes, which are not intended to be highly spectacular like De Mille's—I don't claim to be a big battle director.

Here is an outline of the film:

After explanatory opening titles designed to show the struggle for power between the two opposing branches of the Plantagenets, the film opens with the final scene of *King Henry VI*, Part III (Act V, Scene vii), presenting the coronation of King Edward IV, attended by his brothers, the Dukes of Clarence and Gloucester. At the

THE TAMING OF
THE SHREW
(U.S.A. 1929).
Director, Sam Taylor

Set designs by
Laurence Irving

Set for Final Scene

Costume design for
Douglas Fairbanks
by Laurence Irving

The Marriage. With
Douglas Fairbanks,
Mary Pickford

ROMEO AND JULIET
(U.S.A. 1936)
Director, George
Cukor

Norma Shearer as
Juliet

Leslie Howard as
Romeo

A MIDSUMMER NIGHT'S DREAM (U.S.A. 1935). Directors, Max Reinhardt and William Dieterle

Top left: Ross Alexander as Demetrius and Mickey Rooney as Puck

Left: The Fairies: Oberon (Victor Jory), Titania (Anita Louise)

Bottom left:
Oberon and his train

Above: The Fools: Flute (Joe E. Brown), Bottom (James Cagney), Starveling (Otis Harlan), Quince (Frank McHugh), Snout (Hugh Herbert), Snug (Dewey Robinson), Ninny's Tomb (Arthur Treacher)

AS YOU LIKE IT (Great Britain 1936). Director, Paul Czinner

Orlando (Laurence Olivier), Rosalind (Elisabeth Bergner)

HENRY V (Great Britain 1944). Director, Laurence Olivier

The model of Elizabethan London

The Tiring House at the Globe Theatre

Leslie Banks as the Chorus

Katharine (Renee Asherson), Alice (Ivy St Helier)

Laurence Olivier as Henry V

Falstaff (George Robey), Mistress Quickly (Freda Jackson)

HENRY V

The Battle of Agincourt

HAMLET (Great Britain 1948). Director, Laurence Olivier

Hamlet (Laurence Olivier)

The Ramparts

HAMLET

Gertrude (Eileen Herlie) with
Hamlet

Claudius (Basil Sydney) with
Hamlet

Claudius with Laertes
(Terence Morgan)

The death of Claudius

RICHARD III (Great Britain 1955). Director, Laurence Olivier

Top left: Costume design by Roger Furse for the Lady Anne

Pamela Brown as Jane Shore

Left: The Coronation of Edward IV (Cedric Hardwicke)

Above: Richard, Duke of Gloucester (Laurence Olivier) with the Lady Anne (Claire Bloom)

Right: Richard as King

MACBETH (U.S.A. 1948). Director, Orson Welles

Macbeth (Orson Welles)

Macbeth as King

Macbeth in the Banquet scene. Lady Macbeth (Jeanette Nolan)

The Holy Father (Alan Napier)

MACBETH (Great Britain 1960). Director, George Schaefer

The Witches: April Olrich, Anita Sharp-Bolster and (*above*) Valerie Taylor, as they appear in Macbeth's dream

Macbeth (Maurice Evans) and Lady Macbeth (Judith Anderson) after the murder of Duncan

moment of crowning, Gloucester turns suddenly in close-shot to the camera with a leering smile. The speech, 'Now is the winter of our discontent' (with additions from another, later, speech, and from *Henry VI*, Part III, Act III, Scene ii), follows the procession through the streets, and some symbolic business in which Gloucester's coronet is dropped from its cushion by his page. The total speech, played in a single six-minute take in the large, empty L-shaped set of the coronation hall, is spoken direct to the camera, some parts of it intimately, ironically, in close-shot, other parts, especially those which are almost paranoically loud-mouthed, spoken from a distance, the camera following Gloucester into the other wing of the hall where the King's throne is set, surmounted by a vast, pendant crown. Gloucester asks for our appreciation with his slyly upturned eyes, his knowing nods and glances, and the humorous delight he takes in his own astute villainy. But behind these attractive touches lies the sinister obsession of his megalomania, and the devilish pacing of his crow-like feet, shod in black shoes with long, pointed toes.

Olivier uses a composite set which, like the contiguous sets in a television studio, contract topographical space—the Tower of London lies a few paces from Westminster, and Westminster from the Palace. The action, therefore, can flow unimpeded from scene to scene, wherever in London or its vicinity it may be placed; in fact, time and space are both contracted. The 'delta' of the plot is simplified and channelled as far as possible into a single, broad-flowing river. The episode concerning Clarence, which comes first in the play, is inserted in the middle of the scene of Gloucester's impudently fantastic wooing of Anne at the very moment she is following the body of her husband, whom Gloucester has killed, to the grave. This scene is interrupted at the point when she first shows signs of succumbing to Gloucester's hypnotic powers. Olivier's initial use of Gloucester's evil shadow follows—the interchange between Gloucester and the King, who succumbs like Anne to his suggestions that Clarence is plotting a *coup d'état*, is conveyed by means of shadows, from which we suddenly cut to Edward's terrified face. Gloucester then mockingly watches the proceedings which lead up to Clarence's arrest; he walks with the camera along a corridor looking down through a succession of windows on the mime within, when Clarence is being accused of treason. 'Plots have I laid,' says Gloucester, with a knowing wink.

49

Only after Clarence has been led off to the Tower in deep distress—so leaving, as Gloucester says, 'the world for me to bustle in'—does the second section of the wooing scene with Anne follow, giving perhaps those needing psychological reassurance a little more time to adjust to the ease with which she succumbs so helplessly to his cynical blandishments. Once she has given way, he seizes her with possessive triumph, exclaiming with mock surprise as she leaves him, 'Was ever woman in this humour woo'd?' Then again his shadow intrudes, this time on the floor of her bedroom; her white dress is seen turning slowly towards him within the frame of the shot. Gloucester's shadow recurs for the third time over the spy-hole in the door of Clarence's prison-cell after Clarence's long but beautifully spoken lamentation. Walton's music rather conventionally reflects the deep melancholy of Clarence's mood. The death of Clarence is violent, followed by the harsh visual shock when his body is thrust head-foremost into a great butt of wine.

The continuous emphasis of the production is on betrayal—betrayal of the innocent and of conspiratorial supporters alike. For the purpose of this production everyone whom Gloucester overthrows has at least the appearance of helplessness—the King, Anne, Margaret, Clarence, Hastings, and later even Buckingham, Gloucester's closest ally.[7] Most innocent of all are the little Princes, with whom Gloucester indulges in sinister play—broken only for a moment when the younger Prince, Duke of York, says, 'Because that I am little, like an ape, / He thinks that you should bear me on your shoulders.' Immediately Gloucester's face embodies evil, and a musical chord reinforces this sudden, savage change of mood.

After Gloucester has been crowned Richard III, he abandons any further pretence of goodwill or even ironic humour. This is anticipated in a macabre moment (another of Olivier's theatrical *tours de force*) when the trick designed to make the citizens of London appear to choose him as King succeeds; he slides down a bell-rope and immediately asserts an autocratic authority over Buckingham, demanding an expression of abject allegiance from a man he has hitherto treated as an equal. During the coronation, his head is back to the camera. The camera moves in three stages round the courtiers who acclaim him. Then, with indecent haste, the newly crowned King seizes Anne, his unhappy Queen, and rushes her to the throne he has so long coveted; then, just as suddenly, he forgets her altogether as he indulges in a long, obsessive contemplation of it. He is sunk in a dream of fulfilment. Once on the throne, he sits jutting forward at those who approach him, like a viper about to strike. The sinister atmosphere extends to the smothering of the Princes in the Tower, which is carried out to sweet music and the lamenting lines of the murderers: when Richard's opponents from the House of Lancaster begin to close in, there is a fantastic scene in the Palace, the hall is lit by torch-bearers, while messengers, also carrying torches, bring ill news to Richard, who rages at them like a baited bull. The scene culminates in a great triumphal cry: 'Buckingham is ta'en', with voices echoing through the hall.

The final scenes are on Bosworth Field, rather improbably shot in Spain. The slyly confidential remark to the audience, 'Richard's himself again', seems to echo the Gloucester of old. In the fighting, horses are twice shot from under him, and the crown—the prize-symbol of the film—rolls in the mud, kicked aside by horses' hooves. Richard, alone and unhorsed, is hacked down by a pack of soldiers, and he finally falls, holding up his sword with his two-fingered hand. As he dies, his body seems to protest with violent contortions. The film ends with a long musical coda, with the credits shown on a design which, like the opening titles, features the ill-fated crown of England.

In the mid 1950s Olivier endeavoured to set up a film production of *Macbeth*, in which he had appeared, with Vivien Leigh as Lady Macbeth, at Stratford-upon-Avon in 1955. Of his attempt to produce *Macbeth* for the screen, Laurence Olivier writes:

> I offered the film to Rank on a £400,000 budget, having spent two periods of time for exhaustive reconnoitring in Scotland for locations, with the nucleus of my production team, Roger Furse, Carmen Dillon and Anthony Bushell. We then made the script upon which we were hoping to set up the film. Arthur Rank and John Davis refused me this £400,000 budget, being too much influenced by the new bank rate of 7 per cent to produce this sort of sum. I then went to a variety of people; the early money was easy, a promise of £260,000 from Mr Sam Spiegel and other promises of more, but no hope anywhere of arriving at the finishing money, even from the Film Finance Corporation.
>
> I was never any good as a promoter, particularly of my own stuff. Alex Korda had just died, and I missed him sorely. Del

had at this time disappeared altogether from pictures. I went across to Paris to see one or two of the Rothschilds, and to New York to delve into the clothing trade. After nine months, almost with a sense of relief, I gave the thing up.[8]

The three Olivier productions, spanning the period 1945–55, are still widely shown, though they belong to an era of film-making which seems long superseded by very different techniques of presentation. In certain respects, particularly the studio theatricality of certain settings and the old-fashioned acting style of certain supporting players, they inevitably date. But in other, more important, respects they live as representatives of that great period of Shakespearean star-acting initiated largely by Laurence Olivier himself, immediately after the war. Other, and widely different, interpretations were to succeed the work of this period, particularly in the later Shakespearean productions of Peter Brook, Peter Hall and Trevor Nunn during the 1950s and 1960s. But these three films, each very different in significant respects from the others, represent in themselves a specific era in Shakespearean film-making, and a unique artistic achievement.

Notes to Chapter 4

1. A small addition were the lines from Marlowe's *Tambourlaine* spoken by Pistol: 'Is it not passing brave to be a king / And ride in triumph through Persepolis?'

Analysing the excisions in *Henry V* as a film, James E. Phillips, writing in *Hollywood Quarterly* (October 1946), claims that the cuts are designed to transform Henry 'from a complex and archaic symbol of ideal kingship into the dynamically appealing figure that he is in the film'. In other words, he is being modernized, to suit our contemporary concept of a hero. The 'totalitarian' aspects of his character as a king, as shown in his policy towards Scotland discussed in Act I, and his handling of the plot by Cambridge, Scroop and Grey to kill him, are either cut out or toned down, along with his notorious order to kill the French prisoners of war, or his tirade at Harfleur threatening the city with bloodshed, rape and pillage.

2. The Irish location was Lord Powerscourt's estate at Enniskerry, near Dublin; 180 horsemen and 500 footmen of the Eireann Home Guard were employed for the battle scenes. Of the thirty-nine days set aside for the loca-

tion work, fourteen were lost through rain, and other days were beset with cloud. Rather under a minute's action per day of shooting eventually reached the screen. For the charge, a railway track was laid along a farm road to cover the long tracking shot of the galloping horsemen. The costs of the film are analysed in Hutton's *The Making of Henry V*, pp. 63–6, the total reaching £475,708. Shooting began in June 1943 in Eire; studio shooting at Denham started in August, finishing early in January 1944. Editing and dubbing were concluded by July 1944.

3. For a scene-by-scene analysis of the interrelation between picture, speech, sound effects and music, see Manvell and Huntley, *The Technique of Film Music*, pp. 78–91. See also pp. 110–11 for analysis of the opening music to the film. Sir William Walton's own comments on composing for the Shakespearean films are quoted.

4. Two of the soliloquies were cut in the film version—'O! what a rogue and peasant slave am I' and 'How all occasions do inform against me'. Controversial primary omissions in the film were the characters of Rosencrantz and Guildenstern, and of Fortinbras, the Prince of Norway. The text was heavily cut, many scenes disappearing altogether, such as the scene of the Ghost crying, 'Swear' to Hamlet from underground, and some of the initial scene between Hamlet and the First Player, including the set-speech of Priam's daughter. Among the adaptations made in the text was the reversal of Hamlet's final scene alone with Ophelia and the soliloquy, 'To be or not to be'; the soliloquy precedes this scene in the text, succeeds it in the film. Some twenty-five words in the text as finally used were modernized, for example 'persist' for 'persevere' and 'hinders' for 'lets'. (For the complete list of verbal changes, see Alan Dent, *Hamlet: the Film and the Play*, p. 26.) By far the most serious loss is Rosencrantz and Guildenstern who, as the King's spies, enable Hamlet to throw so much light on his character and situation as he sees it. The character of Fortinbras, representing royal integrity, as well as speed and assurance in action, is another severe loss in the film.

There was considerable correspondence in *The Times* about the textual alterations in *Hamlet*, following a Leader protesting about these which appeared on 12th May 1948. The matter was also discussed in a B.B.C. Third Programme discussion in which I took part with Alan Dent and Philip Hope-Wallace of *The Guardian*.

5. This effect was first used by Jean-Louis Barrault in his stage production of *Hamlet*, and was reproduced by arrangement with him in the film. The

voice of the Ghost was recorded by Laurence Olivier himself on tape, which was slowed down very slightly to give his speech an unearthly quality.

6. Ed. Brenda Cross.

7. Richard, in the context of the whole Henry VI series, was only a villain among villains. For example, Queen Margaret, widow of Henry VI, was a murderess. Shakespeare, possibly to placate Queen Elizabeth, who was notoriously touchy about the murder or deposition of Kings, made Richmond a noble character out of compliment to the House of Tudor—as Henry VII, he was Elizabeth's grandfather.

8. Sir Laurence denies any knowledge of an earlier attempt by Del Giudice to set up *Macbeth* for him, as recorded by Clayton Hutton in his book *Macbeth: the Making of the Film.* According to Clayton Hutton, these attempts, confined largely to the United States, involved an offer of backing from Sidney Kaufman, who was eventually to emerge as the backer of George Schaefer's production of the film version of *Macbeth*, with Maurice Evans and Judith Anderson, in 1960. See below, page 115.

ADDITIONAL NOTE: Laurence Olivier was to appear subsequently in the film of *Othello*. See page 117.

5

Shakespeare by Orson Welles

MACBETH

Orson Welles's film version of *Macbeth* (1948) was a development on
the screen of a production he had already presented at the Utah
Centennial Festival at Salt Lake City. Sponsored by Herbert Yates
of Republic Pictures, with a very small budget of £15,000, Welles
shot the film in twenty-three days during the summer of 1947. It was
his fifth feature film, and was to be his last work in the United States
for seven years; he left for Europe and did not return until 1954,
when he played King Lear on Broadway.

Welles had continual contact with Shakespeare, whom he calls 'the
staff of life', before he filmed *Macbeth*. He had a precocious love for
Shakespeare; born in 1915, it is said he could recite from *King Lear*
at the age of seven. At sixteen he was acting and even directing at the
Dublin Gate Theatre, where Micheál MacLiammóir believed him to
be what he claimed, a leading actor from Broadway; during 1931–2
he appeared in a number of Shakespearean plays in supporting parts.
During 1934–5 he played in Shakespeare with Katherine Cornell's
company, and in 1936 he joined with John Houseman (a Rumanian,
educated in France and England, who had emigrated to the United
States in 1924) to develop the Federal Theatre Project, a govern-
ment-sponsored organization designed to foster the drama and combat unemployment among actors. For the Federal Theatre Welles
produced *Macbeth* in Harlem with an all-Negro cast, changing the
setting from Scotland to Haiti; the witches were played by voodoo

55

witch-doctors. Along with John Houseman, he next launched the Mercury Theatre, which opened with a modern-dress version of *Julius Caesar*, in which Welles played Brutus. In 1938 the Mercury Theatre of the Air developed his reputation still further on radio.

Welles's approach to *Macbeth* was bound to be unusual. First of all, he imposed upon it a theme which has no parallel in the text, and announced it himself at the beginning of the film—much as Laurence Olivier was to do at the beginning of *Hamlet*. The words were spoken over shots of the witches seen amid a swirl of mists at work over their cauldron, shaping the clay image of a baby, which was to be a symbol used throughout the film. *Macbeth*, Welles said, was a story which involves 'plotting against Christian law and order'; the hostile forces were 'agents of chaos, priests of hell and magic' making use of 'ambitious men' to achieve their dark and primal purpose. In order to provide a Christian symbol in the film he created a new character, a priest, to whom he gave lines taken over from other, suppressed characters. Welles cut the play extensively (the film runs only eighty-six minutes); he re-arranged scenes; he even introduced lines from other plays.

The result is a Wellesian superstructure imposed upon the play, which is then bent to conform to this new thematic device; visually, it is often striking and splendid. But the verse is for the most part badly spoken, even by Welles himself. The original track of 1948 sounded, in his view, too American; later (during the production of *Othello*) he re-recorded two-thirds of the track in order to give the speech a more Scottish flavour. The result is that the sound is uneven in quality and often scarcely intelligible, especially as Welles used at times an echo-channel to give the voices a dimension larger than life.

The action is not only changed, but incredibly speeded up. The friar intervenes after the witches' prophecies; indeed, the prophecies are fulfilled immediately after their announcement; the Thane of Cawdor is dragged on, a prisoner, and his insignia handed over to Macbeth, who at once dictates the letter to his wife, whom we then see reading it. Macbeth, riding through the mist, arrives to join her as Cawdor is executed, the axe descending to the beat of a drum. His head is later put on display, spiked on a lofty cross. Macbeth, in fact, embraces his wife while a corpse swings in the background. Here is speed, but there is more to come. King Duncan, a slow, fat man, arrives as Macbeth and Lady Macbeth are still talking, and while Duncan is praising the beauty and peace of the castle, which is little more than a rugged cavern, Lady Macbeth is presenting Macbeth with the drugged drink for the guards. Banquo arrives, and as soon as he is disposed of, Macbeth plunges into his speech of the 'air-drawn' dagger at the line, 'Now o'er the one half-world/Nature seems dead'. As he speaks the line, 'moves like a ghost' there is a quick dissolve to Lady Macbeth bending over the king. There is recurrent thunder throughout the scene in which she drives him to Duncan's room, where his shadow is seen looming over the sleeping man. An owl shrieks, and he starts in fright. While the murder takes place, off-screen, the camera holds on to a scene of the castle cliffs. When Macbeth returns to his wife, his hands ('This is a sorry sight') appear to be suddenly enlarged by being held close to the camera.

Welles frequently uses striking compositions, with violent contrast between foreground and background figures. The influence of Eisenstein (who uses these patterns or groupings with greater aesthetic restraint) is evident not only in the deployment of lines of men with their tall and slender lances, but also in the juxtaposition of the characters in twos or threes, often with a vast head-and-shoulders looming in the foreground of the shot, with the complementary character or characters placed (in near profile, or in full figure at a distance) in the background. A composition such as this follows now, with Macbeth in the foreground and Lady Macbeth in full-figure profile posed behind him. The effect is too beautiful, too self-consciously photogenic, destroying the powerful atmosphere of the moment. As she grasps the dagger from him, the knocking at the gate is heard. Water drips down into the courtyard where Macbeth waits, with great play of his hands in the foreground. After the castle has been roused, we go straight over to the establishment of Macbeth and Lady Macbeth as King and Queen with the line: 'Thou hast it now: King, Cawdor, Glamis, all.' The camera is sharply tilted, the composition becoming again over selfconscious. 'You lack the season of all natures, sleep,' she says, and adds seductively, 'To bed. To bed.' But Macbeth draws the curtain between himself and his wife, and his voice rises to a scream on the words, 'Methought I heard a voice cry, "Sleep no more",' taken from the scene after Duncan's murder.

The courtyard of Macbeth's royal castle is a purely stylized structure, an open area all but surrounded by towering crags; steps lead down into it. Macbeth, wearing a huge, square-shaped, Mongolian-looking crown cornered with spikes, sits enthroned like a god, the silhouette of his head and shoulders filling the foreground of the frame, while all those who speak to him stand dwarfed below in the courtyard. He summons the murderers destined to kill Banquo; the close-ups develop as he dominates them, and over-stylized two-shots, mostly in profile, are used when Macbeth warns his wife of the impending 'deed of dreadful note'. When the murderers bring back their news, the camera is tilted up to show Macbeth either flanked by these agents or alone. As his doubts crowd in on him because Fleance has escaped, he wanders through the dripping caverns of the castle, and finally bathes his sweating face in water streaming down the wall. His voice echoes, repeating his words. He comes to a great butt of wine, which leads him straight into the banquet scene, one of the most effective sequences in the film. His face blenches at the sight of the ghost, and the scene cuts to the astonished, staring faces of the guests. Back in close-shot on the face of Macbeth ('Never say I did it'), he raises his finger, the shadow of which, pointing, takes the camera round until we see the table empty except for Banquo's ghost seated at the far end. Macbeth's drunken face sweats. Finally he breaks up the banquet by upsetting the contents of the table. Then he sits, leaning back against the table —'The time has been, my senses would have cooled/To hear a night-shriek', he says, from later in the play. Lady Macbeth, almost a cypher in this scene, manages to dismiss the guests. This is followed by an impressionistic scene of Macbeth's resort once again to the prophecies of the witches.

The scene with Macduff in England is played symbolically under a great Iona cross, and it is the friar, not Ross, who warns Lady Macduff of her danger and later brings the news of her death to her husband. These are the forces of goodness gathering to overcome evil, and the music of the English scene emphasizes this. Immediately these forces begin to mass in Scotland, carrying their tall, spindly crosses. Macbeth's supporters are few in number; a prolonged shot, which tracks with Macbeth, finally brings him into Lady Macbeth's bedroom. While the armies of Malcolm and Macduff cut down the trees of Birnam Wood, the scene is intercut with those of the army, advancing with their branches through the mist. The sleep-walking scene follows: Macbeth joins his wife again as she says, with an echo of her early seductiveness, 'To bed. To bed. To bed.' He wakes her with a kiss, and she runs screaming from him through a dream-like perspective of pagan monoliths, finally throwing herself over a cliff to her death. Her end is announced as from a great distance against this same vista of monolithic stones. Macbeth utters the speech, 'Tomorrow and tomorrow and tomorrow', against a cloud-scape, with a big close-up as climax. He looks down, a towering profile, on a small figure in the courtyard below, reduced to a pin-head. Seyton, his servant, becomes a dwarf swinging on the rope of the alarum-bell. It is a scene from hell, a hell assaulted now by the battering-rams of the invading armies. After his final struggle and death, Macbeth's severed head is tossed away like garbage.

Welles has described this elaborate re-visualization of the play as a 'violently sketched charcoal drawing of a great play'. He wanted it to be a 'Stonehenge-powerful, unrelieved tragedy'. It was to this end, therefore, that the sets created an artificial world of caves, rock-enclosed areas like the core of an extinct volcano, catacombs and cells with fiercely barbed window frames; it is a world of moving mist and falling water; swine wallow in mud at the castle entrance. Shots are distorted in mirrors to reflect the bent mind of Macbeth. The costumes are part Asiatic, part barbaric, made up alike of skins, cloth and metallic armour. Special effects are used to make the scenes of witchcraft macabre and unearthly.

It is unfortunate that the playing (and the ill-balanced recording) should be so weak. Welles's enormous presence naturally dominates, but like the Shakespearean actor-managers of the past he has been satisfied to surround himself with players who fail to make any kind of mark either in characterization or speech. They seem utterly untrained in the speaking of Shakespeare, misuse the rhythm, and alternately boom or utter inaudible words on the sound-track. Perhaps some exception should be made for Dan O'Herlihy as Macduff and Roddy McDowall as Malcolm. Jeanette Nolan, as Lady Macbeth, was Welles's third choice only. He wanted first Tallulah Bankhead (an interesting choice), and secondly Agnes Moorehead to play the part. Tallulah Bankhead refused, and Agnes Moorehead was already engaged. Jeanette Nolan was a radio actress appearing in her first film; she acted no more than competently, and brought little

59

personality to the part. She utterly failed to match Welles's brooding majesty, his Titan rages, his paralysed fear and superstition, his haunted melancholy. Yet, for all his experience of Shakespeare on the stage and radio, Welles lacked any real mastery of Shakespearean speech. He relied on his uniquely resonant voice to give him command, but his utterance became only boom and mumble, enhanced (as we have seen) by his insistence on using an echo-channel to inflate his vocal effects. As often as not, the verse seems to mean nothing, and we are left with the powerful appearance and personality of a man who is a great natural actor performing in a dramatic medium which requires as much discipline of utterance as it does emotional response.

Technically, the film was shot so as to require the minimum direct lip-synchronization, which is why Welles was able later to re-record a great part of the sound track. It is essentially a film in which the track is largely complementary to the visuals. The film has been called a counterpoint to, as distinct from a counterpart of, the play, Its great visual variety was only achieved in the short time in the studio by having two units working simultaneously on the sets, which were made up of movable sections; to get the maximum number of shots for the final siege of Dunsinane, cameramen in costume were sent into the struggling crowd of extras to capture close-ups with hand-held cameras, carefully keeping their backs to the principal camera, which was filming from a distance.

Welles has said of this film, and of his next Shakespearean production *Othello* (1952), shot in Morocco and Italy:

> *Macbeth* was made in 23 days, including one day of retakes. People who know anything at all about the business of making a film will realise that this is more than fast. My purpose in making *Macbeth* was not to make a great film—and this is unusual, because I think that every film director, even when he is making nonsense, should have as his purpose the making of a great film. I thought I was making what might be a good film, and what, if the 23-day shooting schedule came off, might encourage other film-makers to tackle difficult subjects at greater speed. . . .
>
> *Othello* took not 23 days but four years to make. It did not, however, take four years to shoot. Actually, its shooting period was about the normal one, but there were times when it was

necessary to disband the unit, because I had to go away and act elsewhere. . . . *Othello*, whether successful or not, is about as close to Shakespeare's play as was Verdi's opera. I think Verdi and Boito were perfectly entitled to change Shakespeare in adapting him to another art form; and, assuming that the film is an art form, I took the line that you can adapt a classic freely and vigorously for the cinema.

OTHELLO (1955)

Plans for the film of *Othello* followed Welles's removal to Europe. Peter Noble, in *The Fabulous Orson Welles*, gives a summary account of the vicissitudes through which this film passed, including re-shooting to cover three successive Desdemonas (Lea Padovani, Betsy Blair and Suzanne Cloutier). In all, it took from 1949 to 1952 to complete the film in successive phases, filming in Rome, Morocco (Mogador, Safi and Mazagram) and Italy (Venice, Tuscany, Rome, Viterbo, Perugia). From the actors' point of view, Micheál Mac-Liammóir, who played Iago, published a diary of his experiences, *Put Money in Thy Purse*, which is as entertaining as it is revealing. Welles had constantly to abandon work on the film and acquire more money either from backers or from his own considerable earnings starring in other people's productions. The film was finally released in 1955, reaching Britain the following year.

Like *Macbeth*, *Othello* has a magnificent visual flair, stemming this time not from studio sets but from a brilliant use of the locations. Welles imposed no new or artificial interpretation on the play, as he had done so disastrously in the case of *Macbeth*; rather, he widened its environment by using Italian and Moroccan backgrounds, especially the battlements of the eighteenth-century Arab citadel at Mogador. I first saw the opening reel when Welles himself presented it during a lecture at the Edinburgh Film Festival in 1953. It begins with the upturned face of the dead Othello in the funeral cortège he shares with Desdemona. The deeply vibrating notes of a choral dirge accompanied by powerful piano chords resound as the procession of figures cowled in black moves forward on the battlements, silhouetted against the skyline. Below are the watching crowds. Suddenly Iago is hustled forward past the procession, a halter round his neck, his eyes wild with fear. He is thrust into a wooden cage and winched upwards to the top of the walls, swinging, staring down at his tormentors, and at the funeral procession of the man and woman whose deaths he has caused. The music has grown now into harsh chords echoed by the clanging of bells.

Only after this come the opening titles, and the narration spoken by Orson Welles about the subject of the film, followed by the relatively hurried scenes in Venice before the action takes Othello and Desdemona to Cyprus. It is unfortunate that once again the sound recording is so ill-balanced that the speech is often barely intelligible. The characterization, however, is better balanced than in *Macbeth*; in his old friend, MacLiammóir, Welles had an actor worthy to play opposite him; and Fay Compton made a strong Emilia. Suzanne Cloutier, however, had little to offer but her looks for Desdemona, whom she tries to play with youthful spirit. Mac-Liammóir gives Iago a coldly cerebral villainy; he is a quiet-spoken, Elizabethan Machiavel, who knows how to set about his business. 'I hate the Moor,' he says to Roderigo, at the very beginning of the action in Venice. The temptation scenes, therefore, are effectively played, and had the recording been clearer there is no doubt that the characterization would appear even more detailed and effective than it does with the words sometimes scarcely audible. There is one striking shot, a single long take on the battlements using a jeep to achieve a tracking shot as Iago, walking beside Othello, first rouses suspicion in him as to Cassio's intentions with Desdemona.

Once again, Welles lends his large, theatrical personality to the part of Othello. Peter Cowie, in *The Cinema of Orson Welles*, claims there are some five hundred shots in the film, which runs only ninety-one minutes, and that in consequence the montage is extremely fragmented; the use of dissolves is frequent since appropriate shots were not always there for direct cutting. Again, Welles cut deep into the text of the play, isolating the dialogue and speeches he needed in order to carry the action forward, transposing when he felt the urge. A brilliant touch of improvisation, celebrated by now, was the re-setting of the scene in which Roderigo (after plotting Cassio's murder with Iago) is himself murdered by Iago; Welles decided to film this in a Turkish bath because the costumes for Cassio and Roderigo were not available at the times of shooting. The result is one of the most effective scenes in the film, with Roderigo stabbed by Iago as he hides under the slatted boards in the Turkish bath, surrounded by clouds of steam.

However, the large number of strikingly lit architectural shots coming in quick succession on the screen makes the film restless, and to this extent more difficult to enter into. Satiety sets in; so much photographic beauty becomes a drug. The characters move rapidly, and the camera is tilted upwards to the point of obsession in order to achieve the kind of strictly formal beauty which Eisenstein imposed, more particularly in his last films, *Alexander Nevsky* and *Ivan the Terrible*. Many shots, like those of the massed soldiers in Cyprus, with their pennants fluttering against the sky, could come from these films. In the beginning, Iago and Roderigo, seldom still, watch Othello's movements, now in the Ca' d'Oro in Venice (which becomes Brabantio's house), now from the balconies surrounding the courtyard of the Doge's Palace. The film is at its best when this restlessness is broken and a certain degree of concentration is allowed—when Iago addresses the Doge, for example, with his story of how he wooed Desdemona, who stands listening in the doorway, still rapt in wonder, and joins him to confront her father and the Doge as he concludes the speech. Most of this is covered in close shot. Some of the later interchanges between Iago and Othello are fragmented into a series of emphatically tilted portraits, which drain the drama from the speech, which is in any case under-emphasized, and so transform the scenes into a photographic exhibition. A similar beauty destroys, not enhances, the intensity of the later scenes between Othello and Desdemona, which are posed in a succession of beautiful architectural interiors. The music, too, though often apt, is sometimes used in such a way as to prove a further distraction, disintegrating the dramatic effect. This is particularly so when it is used cacophonously, out of tune, at the moment Othello leaves Iago and launches his first jealous suspicion directly at Desdemona. The music becomes then inordinately emphatic—huge chords resound as Othello's jealous imagination seizes on the image of Desdemona's adultery—'lie with her, on her—'. Suddenly the seagulls are seen wheeling in the sky, and Othello is lying on his back in a fit. Choral music breaks in on Othello's laments for Desdemona's beauty—'She might lie by an Emperor's side—'.

Cutting is often used to great effect. When Othello strikes Desdemona in front of the delegation from Venice, the blow is struck in a straight cut, and is as effective as it is startling and horrifying. In its own way, the scene leading up to the suffocating of Desdemona is effective—Othello, in close shot, pinches out the candle, the contours of his face revealed in highlights against the blackout, his eyes concentrated. It is a play of darkness rather than light. When Desdemona dies, her face is seen faintly outlined beneath the thin veils of the fine cloth that suffocates her. The film ends as it began, with the funeral procession, the chanting, and the dead face of Othello.

CHIMES AT MIDNIGHT (1965)

During 1964–5 Welles completed his third, and by far his most assured, Shakespearean film, *Chimes at Midnight* (*Campanadas a Medianoche*), which he shot mainly on location in Barcelona and other places in Spain.[1] The film was co-sponsored by Internacional Films Espagnol of Madrid and Alpine of Basel, which makes it a Spanish-Swiss co-production. Its cost has been given as £700,000. Welles wanted to isolate the story of Falstaff's relationship with Prince Hal—their strange friendship in the taverns and streets of London and the tragedy of Hal's final rejection of the old man once he had become king. He did this by bringing together the appropriate scenes (and references) from *Henry IV*, Parts I and II, *The Merry Wives of Windsor*, *Richard II* and *Henry V*, and he terms the result a 'lament for Merrie England', a comedy 'viewed all in dark colour'. It is a deeply moving film, in which Falstaff, the central figure, has an essential goodness, even a greatness, about him, which Prince Hal, finally dedicating himself to the formal duties of monarchy and the establishment of power, can no longer permit himself to recognize or even tolerate. Falstaff bears none of the marks of respectability, and Hal breaks his heart by publicly rejecting him. Welles holds Falstaff to be 'the most completely good old man in all drama'. Welles had originally produced a similar continuity of action as a single play with the same title in Belfast in 1960; the title comes from *Henry IV*, Part II: 'We have heard the chimes at midnight, Master Shallow,' says Falstaff to his old friend, the country squire of Gloucestershire.

Before he began production, which was undertaken with some secrecy, Welles made the following statement:

> Falstaff is the best role that Shakespeare ever wrote. He is as outsize a character as Don Quixote. I've always wanted to play him, which is unusual, as there are very few characters

who really tempt me as an actor. *Chimes at Midnight* will be a dark comedy, the story of the betrayal of a friendship. It will concentrate on the actors and there are going to be a lot of close-ups: in fact, it will be my close-up film. The number of sets available to me is so restricted that the film must be anti-baroque, and must work essentially through the faces. When the camera moves away from the faces, it uncovers period settings and actors in costume who are only going to distract from the real thing. But the closer we keep to the faces, the more universal the story becomes.

But, as Pierre Billard points out in *Sight and Sound* (Spring 1965), the film took wing from its locations, such as the little mediaeval villages in Castile and the men and women Welles found there to put on the screen. He began to pictorialize—for example, with Henry V's coronation shot in Cordova Cathedral, using at times a great platform in order to achieve perspective shots. Some of the interiors were improvised in a converted garage.

The film opens with a snow-covered landscape; Falstaff is on one of his periodic visits to his senile friend, Justice Shallow, in Gloucestershire. The two of them sit down by the fire. 'Jesus, the days that we have seen,' cries Shallow, in his cracked and feeble voice. 'We have heard the chimes at midnight, Master Shallow,' says Falstaff, and the film's titles come up with music.

The film is divided into two parts, marked by three brief narrations giving the historical setting; these are spoken by Ralph Richardson at the beginning, middle and end of the film. The opening narration points to the civil wars which disturb the reign of the newly crowned Henry IV; there is a long perspective shot of a high, castellated wall (a background motif of the film), and men's bodies swing from tall gibbets. The narrative identifies the political contenders, such as Worcester and Hotspur, as each in turn passes through a shaft of sunlight in a vast, empty building representing the King's palace; sufficient of the opening scenes of *Henry IV* (Part I, Act I) is left to sketch in the rebellion with which the King has to contend (having, as Bolingbroke, seized his throne from Richard II in a similar fashion) while his elder son Hal, Prince of Wales, enjoys the company of Falstaff, Poins and their friends at the Boar's Head Tavern in Eastcheap.

From the start of the film certain photographic devices become marked. Shooting from a low angle is constant throughout the film; it emphasizes the power struggle between the King—an aloof, isolated figure, his throne set high on a great rostrum, in contrast to the restless, gyrating nobility. Falstaff's vast belly is emphasized by similar, up-tilted shots. Another recurring practice is to use the shafts of strong sunlight which beam down from high windows and make natural, static pools of light in and out of which the characters are deployed. Hotspur's rage at the King ('By heaven methinks it were an easy leap, To pluck bright honour from the pale-fac'd moon—') is taken with a quickly travelling camera which hurries to keep up with his movements; the travelling camera is another constant in the film. He is equally restless in the brief, touching, non-love scene between Hotspur and his wife, before he leaves her to head the rebellion.

Prince Hal is discovered weaving about among the huge butts of a wine-cellar, the camera following him closely through the close, crooked passageways to Falstaff's room. A scene later in the play (when Falstaff has his pocket picked and charges Mistress Quickly to find out who did it, while she pleads with him for settlement of his debts) is now brought forward, and it is Margaret Rutherford as Mistress Quickly who first sets the tone of the film—she remonstrates with Falstaff out of affection, even devotion, never anger. Her voice is fraught with sorrow and anxiety. Falstaff holds court at Eastcheap surrounded by his nondescript followers, the drunks and pimps and whores, who love him for his humanity and his jests. In contrast, all is ice-cold and formal at the Palace, but seething with treachery, resentment and the manœuvrings of those seeking power.

While Hotspur impatiently takes a bath, the Gadshill robbery (with which the play starts) is plotted by Falstaff, who involves Prince Hal in the jest. The robbery itself, a pantomime of movement, is beautifully set among the slender trees of a sunlit woodland; Falstaff and his associates disguise themselves in the white robes of friars; Prince Hal and his close friend Poins conduct their counter-raid swathed in black, putting Falstaff and the rest to flight. The camera, like the white and black figures it covers, is constantly on the move.

The film continually contrasts the lofty formalities of the Palace with the careless, bawdy ease of life in Eastcheap. While the King

Orson Welles as Falstaff. Cartoon by Gerald Scarfe.

expresses his displeasure at the Prince's behaviour, Falstaff returns from Gadshill and boasts of his conquests over the ever-growing number of counter-raiders, to Poins's and Hal's enjoyment. When Falstaff enacts the King so that Hal may practise his answers, the whole tavern gathers to watch as at a play, Mistress Quickly rocking with delight ('O Jesu! This is excellent sport, i' faith'), and there is an echo of John Gielgud's enunciation when Falstaff begins his caricature, wearing a saucepan for a crown. The cluster of whores shriek with laughter. Then Hal takes over as King, reproving Falstaff (as Hal) for associating with 'a devil . . . in the likeness of a fat old man'. For once the camera tilts *down* on Falstaff as he looks up at the boy who will soon be King in earnest. 'Banish plump Jack, and banish all the world,' cries Falstaff, but runs to hide under a trap-door in the floor when the Sheriff arrives to investigate the robbery on Gadshill. Hal covers for him; but afterwards he says he must go to the wars. When the Prince challenges Falstaff's claim that he owes him a thousand pounds, Falstaff replies (and it is the theme of the film), 'A thousand pound, Hal! a million: thy love is worth a million; thou owest me thy love.'

The Prince returns to the Palace to face his father's reproofs ('I know not whether God will have it so—'); the King is remote and distant, raised up on his throne, while the Prince stands below. The first dent is made in his conscience; he promises to mind his conduct, and take his place on the field of battle against Hotspur. Soldiers on horseback pass through the streets, and Falstaff is urged to get men together to fight for the King. He resorts to Shallow in Gloucester-shire, and picks his rustic conscripts in a scene of quiet comedy, lording it over Shallow's chattering and Silence's stutter.

The scenes of battle are finely staged, rather in the manner of Eisenstein in miniature. There are smoke and sunlight, tall lances against the sky, banners and small, decorative tents, galloping horsemen. Falstaff, covered in shabby, unpolished armour, speaks his fatalistic speech on honour while the armoured knights are lowered onto their horses by ropes thrown over the branches of trees. The battle itself develops into carnage—a crescendo of quickly cut details which mount in their savagery against a background of choral music and the clang of metal on metal. Hand-held, swiftly panning cameras, and many un-tilted shots emphasize the bloody violence of

68

mediaeval warfare; some shots are speeded up, and the sequence ends
with scenes of innumerable corpses scattered in the mud. Hal kills
Hotspur in hand-to-hand combat. When Falstaff tried to claim before the King and Hal that it was he who killed Hotspur, there is a
slow exchange of looks between the three of them. (The King is not
present when Falstaff makes this claim in the play.) From now on,
Hal is the more inclined to reject Falstaff, and in the scene which
follows in Eastcheap when Falstaff praises sack, Hal turns away
and leaves him.

The film now enters its second part with the second short narration;
the rebellion is put down, but the King is sick. He is seen lying in bed
('How many thousand of my poorest subjects/Are at this hour
asleep?'). The long speech is accompanied by melancholy music, the
camera steadily covering the King in half-profile ('Uneasy lies the
head that wears a crown'). Falstaff, too, is melancholy in his scene
with Doll Tearsheet, which precedes the fight with Pistol. Doll tends
him after the fight, and their love-scene, played as much for its pathos
as for its comedy, is cruelly spied on by the Prince and Poins. (Poins:
'Is it not strange that desire should so many years outlive performance?' Doll: 'By my troth, I kiss thee with a most constant
heart.' Falstaff: 'I am old, I am old.') But when Hal goes, Falstaff is
deeply distressed, though as if to cheer him, the whole tavern company break into a wild communal dance, like a picture by Brueghel.
At the last, Hal lifts the crown from the King's pillow, goes apart
and kneels. He is beginning to assume authority.

Falstaff goes back to Gloucestershire; the senility of Shallow, the
vacuity of Silence, seem all that is left to him in the male world.
Once again, as they sit by the fire, he says, 'We have heard the chimes
at midnight.' But all their old friends seem to have died—'Jesu!
Jesu! dead ...' At the Court, the dying King revives to accuse
Hal of taking the crown from him before his death; with a sudden
strength, he leaps up and follows him to the throne, where, however,
he dies, reassured that the Prince will become a worthy King. The
rest of the Court watch at a distance, framed in the tall columns of
the Palace. Before he dies, the King admits he himself came to the
throne through violence ('God knows, my son,/By what by-paths
and indirect crook'd ways/I met this crown'). Falstaff and Shallow
are lost in drink, and stagger about happily in a great rustic barn,

69

where Falstaff finally sits to rest: 'Lord, Lord! How subject we old men are to this vice of lying.' It is Pistol who brings him news of the King's death. Falstaff rises in monstrous pride, the camera staring up at the magnificence of his belly: 'What! is the old King dead ... Saddle my horse. Master Robert Shallow, choose what office thou wilt in the land, 'tis thine.' They set out in the snow for the Court.

The new King processes in full panoply, his way lined with soldiers holding their lances. Dragging Shallow after him, Falstaff bursts upon this formal scene, shouting in anticipation of the rousing reception he will get—'God save thee, my sweet boy'. But the King turns coldly on him, looking down from a height. 'I know thee not, old man.' Falstaff is banished from London. The camera dwells on the passing of Falstaff's spirit. Afterwards, he tries to rally: 'I shall be sent for in private to him. Look you, he must seem thus to the world.'

But this is the end of him, as he wanders away through the empty streets at night alone. The camera tracks in on his huge coffin resting on a common cart. Mistress Quickly and his few friends sit in dejection round the empty yard, and she tells them of his passing—'a' parted even just between twelve and one. . . . The King has killed his heart', she says. They push the heavy coffin out across the waste land, covered in snow. The shot is held whilst the narrator closes the film with a brief, ironic comment on the 'nobility' of the King's reign.

Chimes at Midnight is one of Orson Welles's finest films, and one of the most successful screen adaptations from Shakespeare so far made. The much-criticized earlier adaptations of *Macbeth* and *Othello* have the great virtue that they are not reverential or academic exercises— in their best sequences they are pungent, lively, imaginative extensions of the tragedies, flights of fancy too often held back by technical shortcomings, obscurities in the story continuity and incessant over-indulgence in purely visual beauty. But the Shakespearean screen would be much the poorer without these earlier experiments, while *Chimes at Midnight* is nearly, if not quite, a masterpiece.

1. The film was originally planned to be shot in Yugoslavia as an Italian-Yugoslav co-production. Finally, it was set up by Welles's Spanish friends, Emiliano Piedra (a film producer) and Angel Escolano (a lawyer). Welles, in addition to producing, scripting, directing and playing, designed the sets and costumes. He combed Spain for his location—the set for the Boar's Head Tavern was located in the basement of a block of workers' flats in Madrid. The Gadshill robbery was filmed in Madrid's park, the Caso del Campo. One of the villages he chose had twelfth-century half-timbered houses and a church which might have been built in England. The battle scenes were filmed near Madrid.

6

The Russian Adaptations: Yutkevitch and Kozintsev

It is with Shakespearean tragedy, most probably, that English writing has come closest to the taste of the Russian intelligentsia. Shakespeare's humanistic fatalism, his realization that the idealistic impulses in human nature are only too easily betrayed by expediency, his sympathetic understanding of the deep flaws in mankind, give his tragedies a special value and significance for the more serious, sensitive, fatalistic artists of the Soviet Union. At the same time Shakespeare's buoyancy and romantic vigour, which offset his despair, appeal, like the melancholy ebullience of Dickens, to similar emotions so often expressed in Russian literature, drama and music.

The tragedies, therefore, are often presented in the theatres of the Soviet Union, and among the Russian film directors both Sergei Yutkevitch and Grigori Kozintsev are scholars of Shakespeare, some of whose plays have been sensitively translated by Pasternak into Russian prose. Yutkevitch (born 1904) and Kozintsev (born 1905) both began their careers in the theatre after the revolution: they were both associated with an actors' theatrical workshop in Leningrad during the 1920s known as FEX, and influenced by the art of music-hall, the circus and pantomime. It had links with the stylized, expressionist acting current in the German theatre, and with the stylization of the classical oriental theatre especially in Japan.

Yutkevitch, who was also a painter, began his work for the cinema as a set designer, but he became a recognized director while the cinemas were still silent. His early films were to show his strong pictorial sense, and he became a production supervisor in the early 1930s. He completed *Othello* in 1955; in a press interview (*The Times*, 18 November 1960) he said he had dreamed of making this adaptation since before the war, but when Orson Welles won an award at Cannes for his version of the play he had momentarily abandoned the project. However, when he saw Welles's film in France, he was amazed at the difference between his own conception and that already realized by Welles; in the interview of 1960, he said:

> We viewed the play from completely different directions, and our whole approach to its adaptation was different, so that I felt there was, after all, nothing to prevent me from going ahead with my version, and I started work on it as soon as I could. . . .
>
> To begin with mine is an adaptation of Shakespeare's play, while Welles's is a series of variations on a theme of Shakespeare. But more fundamentally there is the almost symbolic difference between our prologues: I begin with Othello's account of his early life and adventures for Desdemona, while Welles begins with the funeral of Othello and Desdemona (and what a superb sequence that is!). I start from life, Welles from death. . . .
>
> I personally prefer the more freely filmic versions to the more heavily reverential. For example, I liked *Hamlet* best of Olivier's Shakespeare films because it seemed to me the most interesting stylistically and the most completely translated into film terms, though I know most purists liked it least.

Othello was photographed in Sovcolor, a development of Agfacolor, which, as Yutkevitch has pointed out, is specially sensitive to half-lights, to the subtle greys and purples of dawn and dusk with which he had already experimented in making his previous film in Albania, *Skanderbeg*, an historical film dealing with Albania's resistance against the Turks. Both *Othello* and *Skanderbeg* end with death scenes staged beside darkening seas at dusk.

Yutkevitch's Othello, starring Sergei Bondarchuk, is romanticized and highly pictorialized, taking every advantage of the spectacular coastal scenery of the Crimea, where the film was largely shot on outdoor locations. Whereas, as we have seen, Orson Welles had opened his film with a sensational sequence showing the funeral procession of the dead at the end of the play, reinforced by powerful, dirge-like music, Yutkevitch opens with a montage sequence of Desdemona's happiness as she contemplates a vast globe rotating on its stand and recalls Othello's endless stories of adventures on sea and land, which are represented by shots of his valour in warfare, his suffering when in slavery, his survival after shipwreck, his mastery of his fate. The music is warm and romantic; after the inset titles there follows the marriage of Othello and Desdemona, isolated in an empty church. It is Cassio who ferries them in a gondola after the wedding. The Venetian setting is suggested by the richly Italianate architecture of the sets and the play of light reflected on the stone walls from sunlit water. There is also much choreographic movement with torches and trailing smoke as Othello is brought out to answer the Doge's summons. When the Doge has finished his enquiry into Othello's alleged abduction of Desdemona, there is a spectacular movement of the characters shot from overhead as they process through an archway to the lagoon; Desdemona drops her handkerchief, which Iago (Andrei Popov) picks up with an exaggerated courtesy, his twisted mouth and prominent teeth forecasting the sinister part he will play. The handkerchief becomes a recurrent motif.

Cyprus is first seen as an architectural location—the massive perfection of the stone sea-walls of the Citadel broken by long flights of steps which zigzag their way up to the highest ramparts. There is a cry of 'A sail' from men on the watch, their cloaks blown out by the wind as they run down from the ramparts. Desdemona is the first to arrive, dressed in black, male attire for her voyage. Iago jealously observes her affectionate meeting with Cassio as it is mirrored in the polished hilt of his sword. Othello arrives, and there is a spectacular crane-shot when he leaps up flight after flight of the stone stairs, his huge red cloak flying out behind him in a flare of colour against the grey-blue evening sky-line.

Yutkevitch's camerawork is often elaborately composed; many shots compass great width of scene, while others involve angles which tilt up to emphasize Othello's towering figure. There is a continuous use of travelling shots. The lyrical atmosphere of the initial love-scenes between Othello and Desdemona is enhanced by their romantic setting of the Citadel high up above the sea. This romanticism is in sharp contrast to the close-ups of the contorted face of Iago, who wants Desdemona for himself; he reveals this plainly in close shots using spoken thought.

The action developing the central plot begins with the drunken fight between Cassio and Roderigo. To the clamour of the alarm bell, they struggle on the stairs. Othello appears and, incensed at what he sees, leaps down to part them. After Cassio is persuaded by Iago to put his case for reinstatement in Desdemona's hand, Iago's evil face is reflected in the water inside a well in the castle. Again his thoughts are spoken, with his lips immobile. His image is finally blotted out when he disturbs the water with his hand.

The panoramic scenic shots on the upper terraces of the Citadel alternate with scenes set down by the sea. Iago first goads Othello into jealousy while they are walking through festoons of fishing-nets suspended by the edge of the waves. As Othello's suspicions mount, he seems to become ever more enmeshed. Finally he is seen striding into a small, white-columned structure—an open circular portico. As his passion rises ('If I do prove her haggard . . .'), so the music grows in full orchestration; music is used throughout the film to establish strong, emotional climaxes; the 'glorious war' speech is even backed by a wordless choral effect. Similarly, the visuals are designed to enhance the words with striking pictorial effects; the mirror-in-the-well shot is used again when Othello refers to his colour ('Haply, for I am black . . .'). The small, circular portico, its shining white marble gay against the blue sky, appears to mock Othello's suffering. Later, the tracking camera follows Othello down to the sea's edge at the close of his speech of farewell to war, leaving both him and Iago posed against a vast anchor; Othello finally falls prone on the sand. When Iago takes his oath to help Othello in his mission of vengeance, the sea washes round them, but the scene in which Othello demands the lost handkerchief from his wife takes place on a small terrace situated on the heights of the Citadel overlooking the sea.

Another original setting used by Yutkevitch is a galleon anchored in the harbour. Iago's gradual feeding of Othello's jealousy is carried further when they are out riding on their horses. When Othello becomes overwrought, he suddenly gallops away alone and boards an empty ship anchored by a quay in the harbour. A big close-up precedes his collapse onto the floor of a deserted galley-room high up on the foredeck of the ship, through the windows of which Iago later arranges for him to watch Cassio receive the suspect handkerchief from Bianca. To enhance the effect of Othello's jealousy, there are lyrical shots of Desdemona sailing on the open sea accompanied by a solitary man—by implication this might well be Cassio. Huge close-ups are used again for the opposing profiles of Iago and Othello when Iago is inciting his master to kill Desdemona.

Romanticism reaches a further stage of emphasis in the Willow Song sung by Desdemona as she prepares for bed; even the strangling of Desdemona is committed to organ music, while Othello's hands are seen bearing down on her neck. The camera pans swiftly to the naked flame of the single light in the room, symbolically blown out by the wind. The images wheel round; a sympathetic gale rages outside, lashing the trees. When the camera finally comes to rest once more on Othello, his hair has suddenly turned white. During his final confrontation with the astounded witnesses, his eyes just as suddenly turn incandescent when he learns the truth about his deception and Iago's treachery. Slowly he mounts the stairs, carrying his dead wife up to the terrace high above the sea; here he kneels alone at the foot of her prostrate body. His final speech is spoken there before he kills himself. The film ends ceremonially, the bodies of Othello and Desdemona lying side by side on a catafalque as they are taken back to Venice by sea, black smoke streaming from the flames of the torches placed around them.

As Derek Prouse has pointed out in a long and perceptive review of the film (*Sight and Sound*, Summer 1956), Yutkevitch sees Othello's tragedy not as primarily one of love and jealousy, but of misplaced trust. The essence of Othello's character is noble; the character of Iago is in contrast ignoble, plausible, malignant, jealous and lustful. He betrays Othello's trust. The climax of the play and film, therefore, comes when Othello realizes that he has been betrayed. Prouse quotes Yutkevitch:

I believe that after the murder of Desdemona the Moor remains calm. The tragedy only attains its climax at the moment when Emilia reveals her husband's lie. . . . The treachery of 'honest Iago' is what finally plunges Othello into chaos. Iago is calm; he has lost the game, but as long as Othello lives he is victor. When Othello raises his dagger, it is Iago who leaps forward to stop him, having understood his intention. Othello's death negates the victory of Iago. The Moor pays for his crime with blood. His courage and his honesty elevate him above Iago. The final wave of Iago's envy breaks forth: he has lost the last round.

Throughout the action, Yutkevitch subtly implies that the net is being tightened round Iago's victims, made all the easier for him by Cassio's evident affection for Desdemona, and hers for him. Sergei Bondarchuk certainly responds to the nobility of Othello; if he fails it is only in his capacity to show the sheer, proud ferocity of the man once he feels himself betrayed—by Cassio, by Desdemona, and finally by Iago himself, the man he has come to trust implicitly. His sudden expression of violence seems somehow out of character, a mere fulfilment of the needs of the action.

At about the same period as *Othello*, an unpretentious production of *Twelfth Night* was adapted and directed by Jakow Frid in 1955, with considerable use of attractive outdoor settings photographed in colour. The text was considerably cut and rearranged, and the character of Malvolio, usually the star part for actors in stage performances using the original, was reduced in scale and status. The general effect of this production is of staidness; though it was acted with great vigour and high spirits, it seems now rather orthodox and unexciting. Klara Lutschko, who doubles the parts of Viola and Sebastian, gives the outstanding performance of the film; she is lively, and full of feeling for Viola's love. Sir Toby Belch and Sir Andrew Aguecheek, however, emerge as little more than caricatures, and were played for broad farce.

Grigori Kozintsev has had a long career in the Soviet cinema, of a distinction equal to that of Yutkevitch; a number of films celebrated in Soviet film history are associated with his name and that of his early colleague and co-director, Leonid Trauberg, and include the silent film *The New Babylon*, and the pre-war sound films *Alone* and *The Youth of Maxim*. Before making *Hamlet*, he also made, among other films of distinction, *Don Quixote* (1967); and in 1967 an English translation of his book on Shakespeare appeared under the title *Shakespeare: Time and Conscience*, containing essays on *King Lear* and *Hamlet* together with extracts from a diary, partly written later, giving his own considered personal reactions to *Hamlet*, which he had directed in the theatre as well as, finally, on the screen. The following extracts from this diary reveal what he hoped to convey in his film, which was made during 1963-4.

The architecture of Elsinore does not consist in walls, but in the ears which the walls have. There are doors, the better to eavesdrop behind, windows, the better to spy from. The walls are made up of guards. Every sound gives birth to echoes, repercussions, whispers, rustling. [p. 225.]

The boundaries that separate scenes must be destroyed. The boiling of life. A maelstrom. No film transitions: no black-outs, fade-ins, or double exposures. The life of government, individual, and military, flow together, merging.

Hamlet's thought penetrates this motley, speeding world, exposes the cancer cells and the decomposition of the organism. [p. 231.]

Working with the designer Virsaladze, we found an important device: the costumes were to be historical only in contour. We rejected quaintly refined period detailing. In other words, a silhouette, but no ornament and no imitation of ancient fabrics. I consider it my great good fortune that this man is working with me. He has a precise feeling for style, and an aversion for historical naturalism. This is important for the plastics of Shakespeare: the generalized features of a given time, without geographical and historical detail. [p. 235.]

They often stage *Hamlet* in modern dress, but tell a tale of ancient life. The tragedy must be played in sixteenth-century costume but must be dealt with as a modern story. [p. 237.]

One of the monologues originated 'on the move'; thoughts alternate in the rhythm of his walk.

The interior monologue will be particularly interesting if it is successful in giving the impression of an explosive force of thought which betokens danger for the government of Claudius. Spies have instructions to shadow this dangerous man, and not to let him out of their sight. And Hamlet unhurriedly and calmly strolls about the room. The camera goes closer; we hear the words of his thoughts, but the sleuth who clings to the door hears nothing. He has nothing to write down in his report: steps, quiet. Hamlet . . . thinks. There is nothing more dangerous. [p. 250.] [1]

I have in mind stone, iron, fire, earth, and sea. Stone: the walls of Elsinore, the firmly built government prison, on which armorial bearings and sinister bas-reliefs had been carved centuries ago.

Iron: weapons, the inhuman forces of oppression, the ugly steel faces of war.

Fire: anxiety, revolt, movement, the trembling flame of the candles at Claudius's celebrations; raging fiery tongues (Horatio's narrative about the ghostly apparition); the wind-blown lamps on the stage erected for 'The Mouse-trap'.

Sea: waves, crashing against the bastions, ceaseless movement, the change of the tides, the boiling of chaos, and again the silent, endless surface of glass.

Earth: the world beyond Elsinore, amid stones—a bit of field tilled by a ploughman, the sand pouring out of Yorick's skull, and the handful of dust in the palm of the wanderer-heir to the throne of Denmark. [p. 266.]

Kozintsev has made other statements about the production. In *Films and Filming* (September 1962), for example, he said:

I think that every classical art changes during the epoch. For every new generation a classical art has a new sense and many new meanings. Now *Hamlet*, in our understanding and in our feeling, is a modern theme in many of its parts. It is quite possible, and permissible, to make an academic production of the play, but I think at the same time Shakespeare needs a kind of new, individual interpretation. Every new effort of every generation creates a new aspect of this character, a new aspect of the history. . . . The general sense of history, the spirit of the poetry, the sense of humanity, should be modern and absolutely lifelike for audiences today. . . . I shall try to show the general feeling, the general philosophy of the poetry, but I shall not use the medium of traditional theatre staging. I want to go the way of the cinema . . . Shostakovich will compose new music for my *Hamlet*. He has composed music for other of my films but for this he has a special interest. We began working together during the silent period. . . .

Many Shakespeare experts have written, and written correctly, that the conception of Shakespeare was absolutely visual, and my task is to change the poetical imagery of the work on to the visual. For me it is not a matter of the appreciation of words, because the translation of this poetry into visual content is the most difficult task in any Shakespeare production. . . . The last translation of *Hamlet*, and maybe the best, is a translation by Boris Pasternak. This I am using as the basis of my script. It is a free translation. . . .

My film will use a wide screen format and black-and-white photography. In *Don Quixote* I used colour because I wanted to capture the quality, the ambience of the warm South; but for *Hamlet* I want the cool greys of the North. . . . Pushkin said: 'Let Shakespeare be your teacher.' He was aware that the general theme of Shakespeare is the fate of humanity in the condition of society based on inhuman conditions. . . . *Hamlet* for me shows the relationship of people in many circles: government, education of children, war, problems of morality and so on. It is a restatement of the true relationships of men. . . .

Introducing extracts from the film at a session on Shakespeare and the film held at UNESCO headquarters in Paris during the quatercentenary year (1964), Kozintsev mentioned again that his primary intention was to emphasize man's essential dignity in a world representing his indignity, and his desire to 'make visible' the poetic atmosphere of the play.[2] He did not, he said, want to use too realistic a castle setting, because the ultimate prison for Hamlet was not made up of stone or iron, but of people. The medium of the film could achieve this more readily than the stage; the essence of film adaptation, he said, is to develop certain aspects of the play which are less accessible to the stage. Actuality, what is photographically 'real' in a film, must be presented as a metaphor, not for itself alone. The ruins of a real castle in the area of Tallin, in Estonia, formed the main location, and the film as a whole took the greater part of a year to shoot.

The following description of the film shows, sequence by sequence, how Kozintsev fulfils the conception of the play; Hamlet was played by Innokenti Smoktunovsky.

A rocky coast; the heavy sound of the sea. A bell tolls, low but insistent. A castle is revealed first of all by its shadow. Strident and threatening orchestral chords introduce the castle itself, with its black flags. A man on horseback (Hamlet) is galloping towards the castle. He enters, dismounts and greets his mother (Gertrude). Sound of gunfire. Once Hamlet is inside, the vast drawbridge is man-hauled into an upright position, with a counter-movement by the descending portcullis. The castle, an isolated stronghold, becomes a prison for all those immured within it.

Claudius's marriage to the Queen is announced by a Crier, the King's words put in his mouth. The first scene in the Court is a session of the King in council; Claudius is hard, able, guttural-voiced; the Queen sensual and worldly. Fortinbras is being discussed; the brief argument with Hamlet, however, is spoken on the move. Hamlet's first solilouqy ('How weary, stale, flat and unprofitable/Seems to me all the uses of this world') is taken as voiced thought, lips unmoving, as Hamlet passes through the crowded room, the camera travelling with him. He is the mature intellectual, isolated in a barbaric, pleasure-loving court.

Hamlet meets Horatio. When he is told about the ghost, the camera keeps in close-shot upon him, with the flames of a log fire burning behind him. (Fire is to be present constantly throughout the film, especially the flames of torches.) The music becomes low and sinister. Troubled, he retires from his friends to the empty council chamber. As he speaks of 'foul deeds', he is seen down the long perspective of the table.

Ophelia is discovered being taught deportment in a hard, formal style by an old woman. When Polonius, tough, scheming and authoritarian, warns her about Hamlet, it is the voice of aged cunning seducing youthful innocence.

It is night, and the Court is indulging in drunken revels. On the battlements, the wind is high. The Ghost appears, a huge, shadowed figure walking on the cliff face; he moves in powerful slow motion, his long cloak extending behind him in the gale. His appearance is heralded by a wild stampede among the tethered horses, which finally break loose. The Ghost is accompanied by sinister music and drum beats. In some shots, Hamlet is seen as a small figure entirely dwarfed by the Ghost in the foreground. The eyes of the Ghost, when seen close to, glow. In the final close-ups, the Ghost can be seen to have fully human eyes. As he finishes speaking, there is a slow pan to meet the dawn, and the castle bell tolls. Hamlet is left lying silent on the rocks by the sea.

Hamlet's visit to Ophelia's room, as she describes it all to Polonius, is presented in mime. Nothing is said. Ophelia runs to tell her father, and Polonius brings the news of Hamlet's madness to the King and Queen in their bedroom. The plot to trap Hamlet through Ophelia is then agreed.

Polonius meets Hamlet on the rocks by the sea ('Have you a daughter?') and again on the ramparts ('What do you read?'). Polonius takes Hamlet's assumed madness to be real. The scene between Hamlet, Rosencrantz and Guildenstern is played with a kind of shrewd sophistication, leading up to Hamlet's sudden question, 'Were you sent for?'

The Players are welcomed by Hamlet in the open courtyard of the castle, while the King and Polonius peer down on the scene from an upper gallery. The chief Player gives the Hecuba speech in the grand manner of traditional tragic acting. Hamlet sits in the Players' cart, which is full of masks, for his soliloquy, 'O what a rogue and peasant slave am I', which is again delivered as spoken thought, his fingers lightly tapping a stage drum. This is followed by 'To be or not to be', spoken by the sea, with some movement about, ending with Hamlet walking up the castle steps, back to the audience while still speaking.

Hamlet discovers Ophelia, left to meet him by the King and Polonius who hide themselves where they may overhear. They push the girl into a large, bare room flooded with light from a tall window. She is discovered by Hamlet sitting disconsolately on the stairs; he sees her as if she were imprisoned behind the bars of the balustrade. There is silence between them. He is angry, suspicious, and he circles slowly round her. He treats her roughly, knowing the King and Polonius are within earshot. He slaps her, shouting at her in a voice pitched high for overhearing.

The advice to the Players is cut, but the play itself is elaborately presented by torchlight on a stage in the open courtyard, backed by a view over the sea. The Court arrives wreathed in false smiles, the procession watched over ominously by a soldier with a gun. As the murder in the orchard is re-enacted, the King slowly rises from his seat; there is a melodrama of screams from the actor playing the murdered King. The cries of the Court rise to a crescendo of music. The King stalks out, and there is chaos as he runs through the galleries of the castle shouting for lights. Hamlet, deeply stirred, calls for music.

The recorder scene with Rosencrantz and Guildenstern follows, very emphatically developed. It is the King's fear (watched in close-shot) which turns him momentarily to religion. He prays, but Hamlet does not appear as in the play. In the closet scene between Hamlet and his mother, Polonius, when he is killed, tears down the curtain which concealed him, revealing, like silent witnesses, the Queen's elaborate dresses set out on their stands. Hamlet treats his mother at first as roughly as he treated Ophelia; the unseen intervention of the Ghost is suggested only by music and the swinging portrait of the dead King in Hamlet's locket.

Hamlet ends by showing his mother some affection, warning her against sleeping with Claudius. Hamlet indulges in wild laughter as he drags the body of Polonius from Gertrude's bedroom.

Rosencrantz and Guildenstern rush about the court searching for Hamlet. He is discovered, arrested, and brought before Claudius. He enters carrying a torch. Guards of sinister appearance keep their eyes on him. He is banished, but he maintains his insolence, walking round the assembly, staring them all out. He goes out, followed closely by Rosencrantz and Guildenstern. He leaves the castle on horseback, watched by a silent Ophelia from a window. She is next seen being locked in a metal corselet and robed in a black dress for her father's funeral. Hamlet, on his journey to the harbour, meets the armies of Fortinbras.

Hamlet boards the ship with Rosencrantz and Guildenstern. The action as he later explains it in the play is fully developed now in mime—he forces open the casket bearing the King's letter ordering his execution in England, and substitutes the letter which will lead to the execution of his captors, Rosencrantz and Guildenstern.

The castle in Denmark is heavily guarded. An iron statue of Claudius is seen. The Queen now shrinks from her husband. Laertes returns, and silently dedicates himself to avenge his father, with upheld sword before an altar. Ophelia is seen alone in the room where she had last met Hamlet; she is dressed in black, and she is mad. Troubled music on strings and horns. Using the balustrade again as a shield, Ophelia is discovered by the Queen. She performs a pathetic burlesque of the dance she was being taught for deportment, and she is left to wander, insane, through the castle.

Laertes and his supporters break into the castle with a clatter of arms. Claudius faces them with confidence, smiling as always, and rapidly wins Laertes over, forestalling this palace revolution before it starts. Ophelia wanders through the massed ranks of guards with their tall spears and armour—a white, crazed, barefoot figure in a framework of metal. Laertes looks on appalled as she sings in her innocence the lustful songs she has somehow acquired.

Claudius is determined to make use of Laertes, with whom he is now able to do what he likes. Meanwhile, Ophelia's body is seen floating in water; a theme is played on strings and harpsichord. The camera lifts to follow a bird flying to the sea. Transition to daytime; Hamlet in the guise of a peasant meets Horatio. A bell tolls.

The grave scene is played for grim humour, which soon turns

serious, though light, almost gay, music sustains Hamlet's examination of Yorick's skull. The funeral procession tops the bare skyline, relieved only by a broken stone cross. The monks refuse to continue with their ceremony since Ophelia is a suicide. Laertes and Hamlet confront each other by the grave.

After Claudius has persuaded Laertes to kill Hamlet, the bird-in-flight symbol reappears as Hamlet accepts the challenge. the duel before the King is watched only by men—no woman is present until the Queen intervenes. The King, whose megalomania is reflected in the large number of his statues which fill the castle, takes little notice of the Queen's death, and little is made of Hamlet's ultimate slaying of the King.

Hamlet, feeling his own death approaching, mounts the ramparts with Horatio. The rest is silence. He dies quietly, lying on the rocks by the sea. The bells begin to toll as Fortinbras arrives. Hamlet's body is borne aloft by soldiers in procession. We look directly down on them as they cross the lowered drawbridge and the portcullis rises. The film ends as it began, with the shadow of the castle, and the wash of the sea.

Kozintsev finished his second film adaptation from Shakespeare, *King Lear*, in 1970, the year in which Peter Brook's version was completed. Once again, the principal location he used was in the Baltic, on the river Narwa in Estonia near the small town of Ivangorod, where he made use of a fifteenth-century castle with its wooden roof. Another location was in the south, a flat landscape in Dagestan, near the Caspian Sea, and there were some background shots from Siberia. The cast came almost entirely from the northern territories, an exception being Oleg Dal, who interprets the Fool and comes from Moscow.

In an interview with Neia Zorkaija, published in the *Literary Gazette* of Moscow in July 1970, Kozintsev spoke of the difference between *King Lear* and *Hamlet*. First of all, *Hamlet* is a monodrama, whereas *King Lear* presents an ensemble. The theme, too, differs widely; *King Lear* is concerned with a civilization which is crumbling through the evils of inequality and injustice. It is a multiple tragedy of deceit; Lear deceives himself, whereas Edgar and Gloucester are deceived by Edmund. Lear is unable to distinguish between truth and sycophancy, and he believes that he possesses far greater power than in fact he does. After his period of self-deception he comes to understand the world of which he was once king. As he draws nearer to the

84

poorest of his subjects, his wisdom develops, and he learns the true nature of society. Such is Kozintsev's understanding of the play.

The differences between *Hamlet* and *King Lear* in subject and nature are reflected in the different techniques of presentation adopted by Kozintsev. Whereas *Hamlet* is exactly set in an Anglo-Danish culture of Shakespeare's own time, *King Lear* belongs to a mélange of periods from the distant past. The art director, Eugene Ene, and the costume designer, S. Virsaladze (whose specialization is costume for ballet), had both worked on *Hamlet*; the whole purpose of the visual presentation was to create a firmly established background to reflect the atmosphere and spirit of the play. The editing style for *King Lear* is more flexible than that adopted in *Hamlet*. The music, composed again by Dimitri Shostakovich, is different, moving away from the set motifs of *Hamlet*, with their well-marked themes. The music for *King Lear* is designed to establish the atmosphere of the film in more general musical terms, reflecting alike the atmosphere and the action. Period instruments are used to achieve particular effects, and there are songs, such as 'Poor Tom'.

This advance information about the film gives a little indication of Kozintsev's approach. But on the strength of his first Shakespearean film, his version of *Hamlet*, Kozintsev, though necessarily working with a translation, has become one of the few interpreters of Shakespeare on the screen to work with a real insight.

Notes to Chapter 6

1. Kozintsev's observations on the King's monologue in Olivier's *Henry V* are of interest.

2. In an article 'Shakespeare on the Screen' (*The Times Literary Supplement*, 26 September 1968), Ronald Hayman considers that Kozintsev has fully incorporated his image of sky and sea into the film, whereas in Olivier's *Hamlet* they are merely adventitious and obvious 'accompaniments', for example in the soliloquy, 'To be or not to be', spoken from the topmost pinnacle of the castle. He considers Kozintsev's film by far the most imaginative of the Shakespearean screen adaptations made up to 1968.

7

The Adaptations of *Julius Caesar*

After the spectacular productions of films derived from Shakespeare sponsored before the war by Warner Brothers and M.G.M., Hollywood, apart from Orson Welles's unorthodox production of *Macbeth* in 1948, fought shy of Shakespeare until the early 1950s, when John Houseman and Joseph L. Mankiewicz respectively produced and directed *Julius Caesar* for M.G.M.[1]

This film, which was released in 1953, depends for much of its effect on a continuous sense that we are seeing recent contemporary events directly reflected in the events of the past. Shakespeare evidently intended the play to be understood politically in terms of the problems of government in his own time—as indeed he intended *Coriolanus* to be understood. Houseman and Mankiewicz in turn intend their film version to be seen in the light of recent experience of the Nazi régime, which had borrowed much of its spectacle and ritual from ancient Rome. Brutus is seen as a rational democrat unwillingly caught up in the need to resist two forms of authoritarianism—first, that being gradually established by Caesar, and, later, the rule of the generals led by Antony once Caesar has been assassinated by the conspirators with whom Brutus is associated in the attempt to rid the state of his threatened autocracy.

The twentieth-century political reference is established from the beginning when the Tribunes, representing the interests of the people, are arrested by the 'political police', Caesar's men. The film then moves straight into the procession in which Caesar, Antony, Calpurnia, Brutus, Cassius and the rest walk to the stadium where the games are to take place—but where, from the political standpoint, Antony is to offer the crown of absolute authority to Caesar in front of the great gathering of the people. The blind fortune-teller who warns Caesar to beware the ides of March is pulled out from the crowd by Cassius and confronts Caesar—who dismisses him as a dreamer. The contemporary atmosphere is struck not only by Louis Calhern's tough, naturalistic performance as Caesar—this piece of casting alone gives the character a modernity of association with American gangster politics—but is carried forward by Edmond O'Brien's brilliant interpretation of Casca's cynicism when he describes, later on, the reactions both of Caesar and the crowd to the offering of the crown.

While these events are taking place off-screen—as they take place off-stage in the play—the great scene in which Cassius draws Brutus into the conspiracy against Caesar is located in a gallery over the stadium, from which every so often the roars of the crowd can be heard. These great roars (recorded specially for the film by a vast crowd attending a baseball game) were orchestrated so that they closely resembled the mass-shouts of 'Sieg Heil' staged at the Nazi rallies. Cassius's bitter allusions to Caesar's growing authoritarianism are given added point by the presence in the gallery of the dictator's portrait bust, to which Cassius makes constant reference as he poisons Brutus's mind against a man he still admires—though, like the rest, he fears what this man he admires may become. After the scene with 'honest' Casca, Cassius leaves, striding through an empty square in which a sudden gale strikes up as, speaking out loud, he continues to plot the best way to bring Brutus into the *coup d'état*. The storm continues into the night when Casca meets Cicero and Cassius in the darkened streets. They are gathering a deputation to visit Brutus at his house. Brutus meanwhile ruminates on the pretensions to absolute power which Caesar represents.

The film follows, in shortened form, the continuity of the play—the scene of Brutus with the conspirators, Portia's entreaties when she is alone with her husband, the scene with Ligarius, and Caesar's rejection, in his palace, of the implications of Calpurnia's nightmare. While Decius is accompanying Caesar to the Senate, an inset scene, with a music bridge, covers the poet Artemidorus's letter of warning to Caesar, who is finally seen approaching the Senate like a gang-leader surrounded by his followers. The conspirators, some half-hidden behind columns, exchange warning glances as they watch him. The heavily orchestrated music gives the scene a sinister weight.

The assassination itself is treated realistically; it is anticipated by the nervous tension shown by the conspirators as they gather round Caesar, who is given his own special prominence by being shot with the camera placed low, angled up at his over-dominant figure. While he rejects the plea of Metellus Cimber, the others close in round him, and at a signal fall on him with their swords. Brutus momentarily recoils from this horrible spectacle, but Caesar, covered with blood, emerges from the throng of his murderers, and in a last dying effort, staggers towards Brutus, who drives his sword in as an act of duty. Their faces, seen in close shot, are twisted and tortured. Caesar falls. A burst of shouting is heard from outside, reaction shots show the anxiety of the conspirators. There is a strong sense that these men are very uneasily feeling their way to power.

A frightened messenger, sent by Antony, edges his way into their presence. When Antony himself follows there is a dead silence as they watch him approach slowly down the long corridor; then they gather round to greet him, but he ignores them and goes to look at Caesar's body. Later, though his words to the conspirators seem smoothly polite, his eyes are baleful. The sounds from the gathering crowds outside seem to grow louder. Marlon Brando, though admirable in appearance for the future demagogue and giving a realistic edge to the speaking of the lines, tends to throw away their rhythm, kicking the words out and shouting far too much.

In the scene in the Forum Brutus is seen attempting to appeal to the crowd through reason. When Antony follows to make his appeal through emotion, the camera is often set low before him, as it had formerly been with Caesar. The visual dominance of the demagogue is introduced, and his calculation on the handling of the crowd underlined. When he descends to come near to the body of Caesar, the blind fortune-teller who had told Caesar to beware the ides of March appears in the foreground of the crowd round the body. The climax of Antony's emotional propaganda is a turmoil of destruction by the crowd.

88

A caption provides a bridge in time into the scene in which Octavius, Antony and Lepidus 'prick down' the names of prominent men they want to have slain, and direful music accompanies Antony's study of the list. The quarrel scene between Brutus and Cassius, the old friends and fellow-campaigners, is filmed largely in mobile two-shot, in which it is Brutus who does most of the moving; the scene culminates in single-head close shots. Brutus speaks as hotly as Cassius, which makes the reconciliation seem to come suddenly and easily. The handling of the revelation by Brutus that Portia is dead is excellent—by expression alone John Gielgud's Cassius reveals his consternation at the news, an exchange of significant glances which is to be repeated when Messala also enquires about her. Brutus appears now to be much stronger and more headstrong than earlier in the film. The boy Lucius's song and the storm that follows, supported by evocative music, build the atmosphere in stylized terms, but the ghost scene which follows is played directly and unpretentiously. The brief scenes of battle, in which Antony's troops defeat those of Cassius and Brutus, unfortunately have something of the appearance of an action during the American civil war—Antony watches his opponents' men marching through a rocky defile, and, with cruel eyes half-closed against the sun, orders the savage attack by his own men, who are waiting in ambush. The film ends, after the scenes of suicide by Cassius and Brutus, with drums and heavily orchestrated music preceding Antony's final lines over Brutus's body, which are spoken in the shelter of a tent.

John Houseman wrote in some detail in *Films in Review* (April 1953) about his approach to the production shortly after it had been completed:

> Our decision, like Laurence Olivier's when he chose to do *Hamlet* in black and white . . . was guided by aesthetic and not by economic considerations. It is possible, under ideal conditions, to use colour for its dramatic value, viz.: the nocturnal camp scenes in *Henry V*. Yet colour continues to be used, in Hollywood today, principally for irrelevant and spectacular show. For all its mass scenes, violent action and historic background . . . Shakespeare's *Julius Caesar* remains, basically, a tragedy of direct, personal strife. Its scenes call for intensity rather than grandeur. . . .
>
> We chose to work in the powerful simplicity of black and

white. . . . Julius Caesar was, generally speaking, designed and executed in monochromes. . . .[2]

While never deliberately exploiting the historic parallels, there were certain emotional patterns arising from political events of the immediate past that we were prepared to evoke. [John Houseman cites such examples as Hitler in newsreels.] These sights are as much a part of our contemporary consciousness—in the *black and white* of newsreels and television screens —as to Elizabethan audiences were the personal and political conflicts and tragedies of Essex, Bacon, Leicester and the Cecils. . . .

In one respect we were fortunate: the action of *Julius Caesar* is swift, concentrated, intense. . . . The cinematic treatment of soliloquies in *Julius Caesar* presented no hazard, for there is none. The words of Cassius as he watches Brutus's retreating figure and plans his next move to enmesh him, and of Brutus in his orchard at dawn awaiting the coming of the conspirators . . . were not treated as soliloquies . . . but as highly charged dramatic speech. [Houseman next enlarges on the importance of keeping the speech immediate and live, avoiding the pitfalls of synchronization.]

For the classic dialogue of *Julius Caesar* it soon became apparent that no such corrective measure could be counted on. The dramatic curves are too long, the tension too high, the speeches too carefully phrased and plotted for them to be splintered, later, into arbitrary fragments. . . . The necessity to secure a perfect and final voice-track *on the set during shooting* added several days to our schedule. . . . Every speech is clear and firm, we trust, with the finality of its original delivery. . . .

We soon found that a Shakespearean scene, no matter how conventionally shot, is not subject to the normal laws of film cutting . . . [We] discovered that a Shakespearean scene had certain general rules of its own. . . . The reaction shot, for instance . . . becomes a tricky thing to use in editing Shakespearean dialogue. Silent reactions, even when carefully planned by the director to fall in predetermined places during a long speech, were rarely used by the editor, who developed a strong reluctance . . . to interrupt the level and cadence of a speech in the mouth of one character by cutting away to the reaction of another. . . . The film, as he worked on it, developed its own proper cutting rhythm and form. The result was no less sharp or dramatic than other cutting—only different. Special problems rose for our chief mixer when he came to make the final composite sound-track . . . perspective, volume, voice-coloura-tion, the balance of voice and sound and music, to mention only a few. Time after time, the conventions of realistic voice-recording and mixing, as generally practised in dramatic pictures, had to give way to a more sustained and lyrical treatment. The Forum scene, with its acoustical and dramatic problems of a single human voice fighting and riding the roar of a great mob, while constantly changing not only its volume but also its relation and perspective to the crowd below it, took days of trial and error and tentative combinations of tracks at various levels.[3]

I am most grateful to Deborah Kerr for giving me the following account of this unusual production from the point of view of one of the principal players:

> I remember so clearly how thrilled I was when Joe Mankiewicz asked me to play Portia in his production of *Julius Caesar*. It was at a time when I only had a series of rather lifeless heroines to play under my contract with M.G.M., and so it was with great enthusiasm that I accepted.
>
> The experience was unforgettable. Utterly professional and startlingly unlike the usual meandering, time-wasting manner in which movies are commonly made. We rehearsed as if for the theatre. All sets were marked out in the rehearsal room, and all key technicians were present at all rehearsals, so that lighting, angles, microphone-placement, etc. . . . all the *technical* facets were worked out before actual shooting took place. Hence the speed and efficiency with which it was completed. The script was shot virtually in sequence, and this obviously is an enormous help to the actors. My scene with James Mason as Brutus was all too short for me! We were so well rehearsed by Joe that of course it was completed in a day! Sadly I wished it could have gone on for ever! But I profited immensely by watching all of the production being filmed.
>
> The sound was all used 'live'—no post-synching, which of course was not too difficult to achieve as nothing was shot outside. It is a great boon to actors not to have to post-synch anything.

Fifteen years later, in 1967, the Canadian producer Peter Snell, with only the documentary *Royal Ballet* and the filmed theatre production of *The Winter's Tale* (discussed below) behind him, started his preparation for making another version of *Julius Caesar* in Britain for Commonwealth United. An initial impetus was given to this production when Charlton Heston, who had a great desire to play Antony again, agreed to do so for the phenomenally low fee of $100,000, plus 15 per cent of the world gross the film might earn.[4] With his box-office seemingly secure with the presence of this star, Peter Snell added Sir John Gielgud to the cast to give the film that other necessity, prestige. The director chosen was Stuart Burge, who had directed the film of the National Theatre's production of *Othello*, with Laurence Olivier, which is discussed later. The total budget finally agreed was $1,600,000, one of the lowest in recent times for a film which involved the spectacular use of crowds, and battle scenes which had to be shot on location in Spain.[5]

It was not until 1969 that Peter Snell finally assembled his cast— the seemingly disparate group of men who had to weld themselves together as a production team, highly conscious of the previous version by Mankiewicz, which haunted them like some unlaid ghost. They were determined to achieve something quite different. Heston wanted to play Antony as a sensual, power-seeking opportunist. During the two-week rehearsal period in London he developed the idea of Antony swaying the crowd in the Forum scene by arguing with them individually at first and so gradually gaining his ascendancy over them as a whole, inciting them to riot. He stood on top of the rostrum steps, the crowd far below him and the great columns of the Forum set towering over him.[6] 'Now let it work,' etc., he claimed, should then be taken as a separate scene immediately following, while Antony drinks wine. Things can take their course. Played in this style, Heston's volatile Antony is in marked contrast to Brando's stolid thug. John Gielgud's Caesar would of necessity be different from that of Louis Calhern. The new Caesar is urbane, and even witty, his ascendancy due to a natural feeling of social and intellectual superiority to the lesser men about him in the Senate. He respects only Brutus, whom he never actually confronts in the play until the final moment of death. Gielgud insisted on retaining many lines originally cut in the script; they must be kept for the sake of rhythm, he claimed, and won his point. He knew the play far better than any of them, and found it difficult to remember the cuts. 'You must not truncate the natural cadences of Shakespeare— nor the content,' he is reported as saying. How often such truncating takes place on the stage, and especially in the films of Shakespeare's plays, so that the organic flow of the verse is entirely lost!

The most exacting problem of interpretation lies always with Brutus, a part James Mason had underplayed in the 1953 version. Robert Vaughn (who plays Casca so effectively) is said to have wanted it; Peter Snell (unaccountably) is said to have wanted Omar Sharif; Orson Welles, approached for Casca, asked for Brutus, but disappeared from the cast altogether in the final stages. So Jason Robards, who had never even seen *Julius Caesar* performed, became Brutus, and determined to give the part a new, untraditional and modern slant—a man troubled by the morality of political assassination. He did not like the rehearsals Burge called prior to the shooting period, and disappeared. He wanted to capture Brutus's dilemmas before the camera, not in the rehearsal room.

The character of Brutus is the key to the play, its centre of gravity. All the other characters, important though they may be in their own right—as Caesar, Cassius, Antony, Casca and Octavius undoubtedly are—must be seen in their relationship to, or effect upon, this central figure, this stoic philosopher, a reluctant conspirator who accepts the necessity for violence against his friend, Caesar, only because he feels it is for the ultimate good of Rome. Any production without a strongly orientated personality playing Brutus will founder, leaving the centre of the stage to what are really only the secondary, though more 'showy' characters of Caesar, Antony and Cassius. The actor who plays Brutus cannot be 'showy'; he must establish his central position to the play through his display of an inner strength which outshines the more rhetorical strength of the showmen. This is what the play is about, and it needs an actor of the calibre (and experience in Shakespeare) of a Paul Scofield to make this apparent at every instant in the action—he must radiate his point of view (mistaken or otherwise) throughout the total length of the play, dominating the conspiracy once he is drawn into it. That he fails, because he functions above the level of mere opportunism and unscrupulousness which guide the power-politicians on both sides, is the measure of the tragedy in the play. It is the reason for his comparative failure in dealing with the crowds in the Forum, not from any inability to sway them momentarily by the weight of reason (Shakespeare gives him a highly rational speech in prose to deliver, and the crowd responds to it), but because he does not realize that in loosing Antony to them he is selling them to the devil and the rule of unreason. But, for the play's sake, Brutus must be acted throughout from strength; the primary part to cast, therefore, is not Antony (the old actor-manager's dream because of its egocentric showmanship), but Brutus. And it was in the casting of Brutus that the film foundered.

Jason Robards is an actor of considerable personality, and his approach to the part had a serious, if perhaps over-contemporary slant pitched well below the level of the character.[7] The very naturalism he imposed on the delivery of the verse robs Brutus of the august power which he should increasingly reveal as the action develops. Robards brings to the part the worried intensity of Edward R. Murrow (whom he closely resembles) in his famous telecasts exposing Senator McCarthy. His Brutus is undoubtedly a good man, but he is not a great one. This largeness of nature must emerge in the two significant scenes between Brutus and Cassius; in the first, Cassius, the able opportunist, uses his debating skill to work on the great man's conscience, and in the second, he vents his barely controlled rage against the almost priggish coldness and aloofness of Brutus when he, too, feels his stoic calm giving way to anger. In the second of these scenes Robards quarrels as hotly as Cassius, and the whole point of the contrast between these men is lost. In the first, he merely appears worried. Although he obviously brings thought to the part, he gives it no stature. So once again, the central character goes by default, and the audience is left with the histrionics to carry the film through—Charlton Heston's splendid Forum scenes, for example, or the excellently choreographed assassination of Caesar, in the Senate, with man after man going in for the kill until, when Brutus (still looking worried) has stopped, they all descend on the dying man and cut him to pieces to louder chords of music. It is a holocaust, and the rest of the Senate huddle together terrified at the spectacle. An overhead shot shows the conspirators encircling the body, bathing their hands ritually in Caesar's blood.

There are several imaginative touches in the film—Antony's spoken thoughts ('If then thy spirit look upon us now,/Shall it not grieve thee dearer than thy death,/To see thy Antony making his peace—') as he shakes the blood-stained hands of the assassins.

Calpurnia's dream with Caesar's statue running blood, and the warnings of the poet Artemidorus incorporated in it, and the fact that the conspirators appear before the crowds in the Forum after the assassination with Caesar's blood still red on their hands. The Forum scene, therefore, Caesar's 'funeral', takes place almost within minutes of the killing—wrong, no doubt, in terms of chronology, but most effective dramatically, and exactly as Shakespeare's text has it. There is much to be said in favour of many aspects of this film, in spite of the stresses and strains of its economies, which show here and there. But it lacks its real heart—the greatness of Brutus, the idealist unable to prevail in a world governed by opportunism.

Notes to Chapter 7

1. I met Joseph L. Mankiewicz in New York while recording a broadcast in 1952, and he was already preparing then for this production. He said that he was excited by the opportunities for contemporary political reference which *Julius Caesar* offered.

2. It is ironic that in 1970, when Peter Snell's film production of *Julius Caesar* was about to be released, M.G.M. reissued the 1953 version blown up to 70 mm. and tinted sepia.

3. For a detailed account of the structure of the music score written by the composer, Miklos Rozsa, see *The Technique of Film Music*, by Roger Manvell and John Huntley, pp. 113–18 and pp. 121–2.

4. In 1969 Charlton Heston, after arriving in London to work in Peter Snell's production of *Julius Caesar*, met the press to introduce extracts from an enterprising American film version of the play made in 1949 by David Bradley, a student of Northwestern University; Heston, also then a student at this University, played Antony; he had acted as costume designer for David Bradley's previous Shakespearean film production of *Macbeth* (1946). The costs of these films were: *Macbeth*, $5,000; *Julius Caesar*, $15,000. In addition to producing, directing and editing *Julius Caesar*, David Bradley played Brutus. Like *Macbeth*, the film made brilliant use of locations in and around Chicago, but made greater cinematic than Shakespearean sense, though Charlton Heston's capacity as an actor was already apparent in his performance as Antony. In 1965, when fully established as a star, Heston ap-

peared in the title role of another, far more mature, production by David Bradley, a screen adaptation of Ibsen's *Peer Gynt*. For a fuller account of Bradley's earlier *Macbeth* and *Julius Caesar* see Meredith Lillich's article, 'Shakespeare on the Screen' (*Films in Review*, June–July 1956).

5. An exceptionally frank, long and revealing diary of this production by Sharmini Tiruchelvam was published in the *Daily Telegraph Magazine* (6th February 1970). I owe several details given here to this article.

6. According to the article by Sharmini Tiruchelvam cited above, Charlton Heston, after returning to the States, sent a detailed letter to Peter Snell explaining how he wanted the Forum scene to be edited.

7. Sharmini Tiruchelvam, in the article already cited, suggests that Robards's close friendship with Robert Kennedy greatly influenced the attitude to political assassination which he tried to reflect in Brutus.

8

The Italians and Shakespeare: Castellani and Zeffirelli

The audience at the Venice Film Festival of 1954 who rose to acclaim the first showing of Castellani's Italianate version of *Romeo and Juliet* were not applauding it because it was Shakespeare. They saw it as a splendidly colourful reincarnation of fifteenth-century Italy in Technicolor, the period to which the play was moved forward so that the more splendid resources of art could be drawn upon for costumes, settings and locations. In this they were right—the film is nothing if not fifteenth-century Italy brought to highly active life on the screen. It was inevitable it should win the Grand Prix for that year at Venice. The story of Romeo and Juliet, or rather of Juliet and Romeo (the Italian title for the film is *Giulietta e Romeo*), is as well known in Italy as Shakespeare has made it in Britain, and there were few present in the audience at Venice who cared one way or the other whether the film kept reasonable faith with Shakespeare. The film was splendidly photographed by Robert Krasker.[1]

Castellani was quite frank about it. At a meeting organized in London by the British Film Academy, he admitted with unabashed frankness that where a scene needed for continuity might be lacking in the play (the most substantial case of this was in a scene added for Friar Laurence) he was quite prepared to supply one—though 'additional dialogue by Renato Castellani' was not included among the credits. Anything which held up the essential action was as far as possible pruned away; lines were cut without attention to rhythm, and speeches (regardless of their 'fame') were quite simply lost;

for example, Mercutio's Queen Mab speech and Juliet's opening speech in Act II, Scene ii. Whole scenes were dropped; for example, the scene with the apothecary. On the other hand, many changes of scene had a new beauty of their own. The marriage of the young lovers is seen through an iron grille, while a Mass is being sung in the background.

With so much attention being paid to the décor, it is small wonder that few people concerned with the production seemed to bother with the script. Adapted by Castellani himself, his only concession to stardom was to miscast Laurence Harvey as Romeo, and to the classical English theatre to cast Dame Flora Robson as the Nurse. At least Flora Robson valiantly stood up for Shakespeare, urging on her director the need for attention to what was left of the original lines, and helping the young and inexperienced Juliet (Susan Shentall) with the speaking of the verse. Susan Shentall had been cast because she was the right age and, in costume and make-up, the living embodiment of a fifteenth-century portrait. No one denied her beauty though everyone was embarrassed by her inability to come within speaking distance of Juliet, that most difficult of parts even for the most experienced actress. The only character who genuinely thrived was Friar Laurence; the part was expanded into a major role in the story, and played with a quiet sincerity by Mervyn Johns. Flora Robson, on the other hand, played down the vulgarity of the Nurse so that she became a thoroughly respectable retainer in the Capulets' service. Laurence Harvey, an excellent actor in the right range of parts, never seemed to come to terms with Romeo; Castellani's aim was to avoid all poetry of speech and persuade his actors to speak naturalistically—Shakespeare, in fact, was a liability which he, an Italian neo-realist, had to overcome, an unfortunate heritage from the British wing of the film production sponsorship. Amid this naturalism, and with a very muted Juliet, Laurence Harvey tried to put up a star performance, with the result that his miscasting became more evident. Only the voice of Sir John Gielgud, speaking the Prologue, gave Shakespeare full utterance in the romantic style.

It was Sir Laurence Olivier who spoke the prologue and epilogue to the second Anglo-Italian production, that by Franco Zeffirelli in 1968. In effect, this version is an up-dating by Zeffirelli in his own fluid, nervous style in stage and film production of what Castellani had aimed at achieving fifteen years earlier; that is, to use the play as a starting-point for an excursion into fifteenth-century Italy in which everything is done to beautify the appearance and enliven the action at the expense of Shakespeare's dramatic poetry. Once again, the street fights were vigorously done, though with the highly mobile camerawork of the fashionable ciné-vérité school. Zeffirelli's emphasis is on youth, on first love, on the tribulation of adolescent innocence sacrificed to the evil rivalries of maturity; careless of the lines, he gave the parts of Romeo and Juliet to two attractive new-comers, Leonard Whiting (aged sixteen) and Olivia Hussey (aged fifteen) with little thought as to whether they could compass the poetry or not. However, the gain was that they looked the parts in the eyes of contemporary youth in the audience, while the rest of the cast was once again induced to play as naturalistically as possible— especially Milo O'Shea as Friar Laurence (again emphasized because of his importance to the machinery of the plot) and Pat Heywood, who as the Nurse gave a splendidly bawdy twist to the character. The action, whether fighting or dancing, making love, or simply moving from place to place, had pace and fluidity—but the play's extrava-gances of plot (if taken realistically, which was never Shakespeare's intention or interest) became over-stressed in a treatment that neces-sarily substitutes the speed and excitement of action and the beauties of costume and location for the romantic essence of poetry which characterizes this comparatively early work by Shakespeare.

Far more successful, partly because the fate of the text matters less, was Franco Zeffirelli's earlier adaptation of *The Taming of the Shrew* (1966) in an American-Italian production jointly produced by himself, Richard Burton and Elizabeth Taylor; the script was prepared partly by Zeffirelli, assisted by Britain's Paul Dehn and Italy's Suso Cecchi D'Amico, both experienced screenwriters. This put all the emphasis on comic, bravura acting—with some brilliant casting, especially Michael Hordern's Baptista, almost on the verge of a nervous breakdown through his daughter's behaviour, and Cyril Cusack's sly Grumio. The interplay of Richard Burton's Rabelaisian Petruchio and Elizabeth Taylor's wildly termagant Katharina was in the spirit of *Who's Afraid of Virginia Woolf?* To allow for these extended slanging matches, the Bianca-Lucentio subplot all but disappears, while the wedding (which has no action in the play, only a description) is developed into a full-scale burlesque, Petruchio arriving hours late, drunk and disorderly. The Panavision Technicolor photography and the art direction are beautiful, but no one from the first was meant to take this film as anything but a farcical romp adapted for the cinema's most celebrated couple.

Notes to Chapter 8

1. Considerable detail on the art direction for this film is given in an article by Meredith Lillich in *Films in Review* (June–July 1956). The locations included the Ca d'Oro in Venice (for the balcony and ballroom scenes), the cloister of San Francesco del Deserto in Venice (for the monastery scenes), the Piazza del Duomo in Siena (for the Romeo-Tybalt duel, with an artificial fountain set in the middle), the walls of twelfth-century Montagnana (for the opening scene with Friar Laurence, who is discovered gathering herbs), the San Zeno Maggiore, with its bronze door and huge interior (for certain of the later scenes). The paintings of Uccello, Piero, Botticelli and many other painters were drawn on for costumes and properties: for example, Juliet's ball dress came from Botticelli's 'Wedding of Nostagio degli Onesti'. Lady Capulet's appearance and style derived from the figure of the Empress Helena in Piero's fresco of the Holy Rood in Arezzo. The fresco in Friar Laurence's cell is a replica of Fra Angelico's work in the Convent of St Lorenzo in Florence. More than this, certain camera set-ups were derived directly from established works of art: e.g., the five boys singing at the Capulet Ball reproduced the group from the Lucca della Robbia gallery in Florence; a portrait shot of Juliet at the ball is copied from Veneziano's 'Portrait of a Young Lady', while Capulet in his study reproduces Raphael's portrait of the Pope. For many other examples see Meredith Lillich's article.

9

Akira Kurosawa's *Macbeth, The Castle of the Spider's Web* (1957)

The Castle of the Spider's Web (*Kumonosu-Djo*, renamed *The Throne of Blood* in the English-titled version) is one of Akira Kurosawa's most disciplined and powerful films. Kurosawa was among the group of younger directors whose talent became marked in the difficult years immediately following the war, and who turned their faces against the traditional, hide-bound techniques of the highly conventional Japanese cinema. Kurosawa in particular faced certain of the post-war problems of Japanese society in such films as *Scandal* (1950) and *Living* (1952). Although radically influenced by dynamic, westernized styles in film-making (particularly those of America), he was equally interested in bringing a new treatment to the traditional, period subjects familiar in Japanese cinema, and it was his film *Rashomon* (1950), set back in twelfth-century Japan, which first opened the eyes of audiences in the West to the potentialities of Japanese film-making. It won the Grand Prix at the Venice Film Festival in 1951. In an earlier film, *The Men Who Tread on the Tiger's Tail* (1946; released 1953), Kurosawa had experimented with the stylized form of Kabuki, the traditional Japanese drama originating in the seventeenth century, though in a form which tended to parody its style. His unexpected success in Venice consolidated his prestige in Japan, and he was allowed to make two films with unusually large budgets—*The Seven Samurai* (1954) and *The Castle of the Spider's Web* (1957), adapted from Shakespeare's *Macbeth*, and drawing directly upon the even older Noh tradition in classical Japanese drama.[1]

Michizo Toida, an authority on the Noh drama, has commented on the introduction of certain aspects of Noh stylization into *The Castle of the Spider's Web*:

> It is found in the scene in which Isuzu Yamada as Lady Macbeth walks with dragging feet and sits with one knee raised, and also found in the musical accompaniment of the Noh in the scene in which Toshiro Mifune, as Macbeth, goes from one room into the other to attempt the murder of his lord, while Isuzu Yamada, left alone, and filled with both uneasiness and expectation, walks up and down the room. Similarly, it is in the tradition of Kurozuku that the witch prophesies with her spinning wheel; the costumes of the murdered warriors are also in the tradition: all of them wear short 'Happi' or half 'hansetsu' coats.

When Tadao Sato,[2] the Japanese film critic and historian, interviewed Kurosawa on *The Castle of the Spider's Web*, the nature of his particular interest in the subject of Macbeth and its link in his mind with the samurai and Noh traditions were developed further:

SATO: Why did you adapt Shakespeare's *Macbeth*?

KUROSAWA: During the period of civil wars in Japan, there are plenty of incidents like those portrayed in *Macbeth*. They are called *ge-koku-jo*.[3] Therefore, the story of *Macbeth* appealed very much to me, and it was easy for me to adapt it.

SATO: What did you intend to represent in *Macbeth*?

KUROSAWA: The images of men who lived through the age when the weak became a prey for the strong are highly concentrated. Human beings are described with great intensity. In this sense, I think there is something in *Macbeth* which is common to all other works of mine.

SATO: Could you explain what kind of Japanese speech has been used for the dramatic verse of Shakespeare?

KUROSAWA: Well, to some extent it is stylized prose from contemporary Japanese. If it had been completely stylized, it would have been too difficult to understand. So I preferred to take a medium line. Where I introduce some verse-style, I have linked it to the traditional style of the Noh songs.[4]

SATO: In *The Throne of Blood* (or *Kumonosu-Djo, The Castle of the Spider's Web*), the influence of the Noh is evident. Did you from the start develop your adaptation with the style of the Noh in mind?

KUROSAWA: In the case of the witch in the wood, I planned to replace it with an equivalent to the hag which appears in the Noh play named *Kurozuka*. The hag is a monster which occasionally eats a human being. I realized if we were to search for an image that resembles the witch of the West, nothing exists in Japan other than this. The other parts, however, I went on developing during the actual stage of interpretation.

SATO: What kind of influence does the Noh play have in *Throne of Blood*?

KUROSAWA: Drama in the West takes its character from the psychology of men or circumstances; the Noh is different. First of all, the Noh has the mask, and while staring at it, the actor becomes the man whom the mask represents. The performance also has a defined style, and in devoting himself to it faithfully, the actor becomes possessed. Therefore, I showed each of the players a photograph of the mask of the Noh which came closest to the respective role; I told him that the mask was his own part. To Toshiro Mifune who played the part of Taketoki Washizu (Macbeth), I showed the mask named Heida. This was the mask of a warrior. In the scene in which Mifune is persuaded by his wife to kill his lord, he created for me just the same life-like expression as the mask did. To Isuzu Yamada who acted the role of Asaji (Lady Macbeth) I showed the mask named Shakumi. This was the mask of a beauty no longer young, and represented the image of a woman about to go mad. The actress who wears this mask, when she gets angry, changes her mask for one the eyes of which are golden-coloured. This mask represents the state of an unearthly feeling of tension, and Lady Macbeth assumes the same state. For the warrior who was murdered by Macbeth and later reappears as an apparition, I considered the mask of the apparition of a nobleman of the name of Chujo to be becoming. The witch in the wood was represented by the mask named Yamanba.

SATO: Noh is virtually a motionless performance, and yet you are commonly known to favour vehement movement. Why do you like the Noh?

KUROSAWA: People in general think the Noh is static. It is a misunderstanding. The Noh also involves terribly violent movements resembling those of an acrobat. They are so violent that we wonder how a man can manage to move so violently. The player capable of such an action performs it quietly, hiding the movements. Therefore both quietness and vehemence co-exist together. Speed means how fulfilled a certain period of time is. The Noh has speed in such a sense.

SATO: What points mattered most in the photography? I feel the influence of traditional Japanese art in the compositions.

KUROSAWA: As I had once been a painter, I am specially familiar with the traditional pictures of Japan. The composition of leaving a large area white and drawing persons and things only within a limited section of the space is peculiar to Japanese art. The influence of such pictures goes deep with us, and comes out spontaneously in our arrangement of composition. The camera work was very difficult because there were many full shots, and the shooting was carried out while I gave strict directions about the poses of the characters. If the actors moved into an incorrect position, the balance of the picture was broken. If a single shoulder went out of frame, everything was ruined.

SATO: Did you design the sets with the Noh specially in mind? I think the room in which Macbeth murders the king resembles the Noh stage closely. Yet as the Noh drama originated in the age of civil wars which formed the background to this film, the Noh might have provided the common style for the sets.

KUROSAWA: That's so. Historically, the castles of those days were in this style. When I went into the way castles were constructed in those days, some of them made use of the wood which was grown as if it had been a maze. Therefore, the wood was named 'the wood of spiders' hair', meaning the wood that catches up the invaders as if in a spider's web. The title *The Castle of the Spider's Web* (Kumonosu-Djo) came to me in this way.

Tadao Sato claims that Kurosawa is more concerned in this film with choreography in the Noh tradition than with the psychology of his characters. He gives several instances of this; for example, in the scene of the murder of the Lord (Duncan), Asaji (Lady Macbeth) walks dragging her feet so that the sound of her silk kimono is heard on the wooden floor to the accompaniment of Noh-style instrumentation. She stands, too, in a familiar Noh posture, with her head bent and her face made up like a mask. The characters frequently stand or sit staring into space, communicating neither with each other nor with the audience—a pose familiar in Noh, as well as in Japanese painting, when the characters are looking deep into their inner consciousness. Macbeth, returning from the murder-chamber, stamps rhythmically on the floorboards, revealing his fear through the sound of his feet. Both Taketoki Washizu (Macbeth) and Asaji are controlled by fate, fulfilling the pattern of a prescribed destiny, controlled by supernatural powers. This, too, is familiar in Noh. Much use is made in the film of mist and rain—a tradition in both Chinese and Japanese art, where fog symbolizes what is hidden and mysterious. The violences of nature recur as motifs in many of Kurosawa's films, as they do in *The Castle of the Spider's Web*. Tadao Sato also reminds us that Kurosawa began his career as a painter, and that this shows itself repeatedly in the beauty of his images, and the play of light in mist and sunshine.

Here is an extract from the script of the film, part of the sequence of the murder of the Lord (Duncan):

> The scene in the Unopened Chamber—Taketoki Washizu is sitting alone in the centre of the room. Each time the flame of the candle stirs, the shadow of Taketoki moves. There is an air of gloom—Taketoki's glaring, bloodshot eyes stare.
>
> The dark-coloured traces of bloodshed upon the wainscot— Taketoki turns his eyes away, yet on the very wood of the floor from which he averted his eyes the outline is suggested of a strange figure which the blood has drawn. Suddenly Taketoki rises impatiently to his feet; but he remains standing motionless, looking to the side. Asaji, with a spear in her hands, enters quietly. Taketoki is staring at Asaji lost in a trance. Asaji, approaching Taketoki, forces him to take hold of the spear. At the same time, the two stare at each other, pale.
>
> The sky—an owl with its sharp cry flies across the crescent moon, which looks like a sickle.

In the Unopened Chamber—Taketoki looks up to the sky, and staring for an instant at Asaji with a strange smile, walks from the room uncertainly.

Asaji—seeing him go, sits down quietly, and keeps quite still in the same pose.

—A long interval—

Taketoki comes back with a ghastly look; splashed with blood, he stands with the spear like a stick, and sits down. Asaji wrests the spear from Taketoki's hands and goes out.

In front of the Chamber—Asaji appears, and eases the blood-smeared spear into the hands of the sleeping warrior.

In an outstanding article on the film contributed to *Sight and Sound* (Autumn 1965), J. Blumenthal comes to the heart of the problem of Shakespearean adaptations. This is arguably the best essay yet written on the subject. He sees *The Castle of the Spider's Web* as a film masterpiece in its own right precisely because it does not attempt to adapt Shakespeare's play to the screen through its *text*. He acknowledges that incidental beauties may occur in the adaptations by such masters of the theatre as Laurence Olivier, or even in the visual theatricalities of Orson Welles, but in Welles's *Othello* (which he prefers to Welles's *Macbeth*) he thinks 'the cinematic flourishes are gratuitous', providing a sugar-coating of striking photographic compositions or dramatic cutting which do nothing to deepen the experience of Shakespeare's play, because they do not represent any real, filmic expression of it. Kurosawa's transmutation of *Macbeth* is a radical one; he 'relies on Shakespeare only as a scenarist whose vision is consonant with his aim, and never as a master of pentameter', which can only too easily become ludicrous on the screen.

Kurosawa's characters speak 'only when they can't communicate in any other way'. Washizu, in fact, is barely articulate, but this does not prevent him from undergoing the same broad experiences as Macbeth, a character who communicates through poetic speech. Washizu 'thinks in another medium'. And so does Kurosawa, who conveys meaning 'by the manipulation of material reality'. The woodlands, the forests, the horses, so immediately responsive to the same supernatural terrors as Macbeth, become the central imagery through which the theme of the film is expressed. 'The forest is

Washizu's mind', a 'labyrinth' (Kurosawa's word) in which Washizu is constantly lost. 'I must paint the forest with blood.' This forest, with its demon witch, takes charge of the action, imbues it with meaning in a manner which makes the sets in *Henry V* appear mere backdrops. In the action, the men and their horses become a violent tumult, time and again returning to the fatal woodlands in which they are always lost and terrified. 'Film narrative depends on the material components of the world being depicted'; the theatre depends on the power of what is uttered by the actors.

Blumenthal puts far greater stress on Kurosawa's inner characterization of Asaji and Washizu than Sato does. This is revealed by their overt behaviour, seldom by what they say. Washizu has a 'vivid but treacherous imagination', but this is never revealed by what he says, which is 'a barrage of gasps, grunts, shrieks, and snorts', expression of the hero's 'primitive physicality'; 'the delicate Japanese architecture is used throughout as a sounding board for the man's tremendous violence ... the spirit of Macbeth [is] distilled to almost pure irrationality'. So also with Asaji. She barely speaks, but 'she is endowed instead with a purely physical power'. Kurosawa's brilliant contribution to Shakespeare's central situation is first of all to make the childless Asaji pregnant, and then make her miscarry as a direct result of the fear she endures once Washizu has taken over his murdered Lord's title and turns to killing and more killing.

The Castle of the Spider's Web, therefore, is a transmutation, a distillation of the *Macbeth* theme, not an adaptation. It is by far the most complete and satisfying of its kind; it is, in fact, unique. It is the work of a man who is a film-maker first and last, and yet this film has won the praise of those whose own efforts have lain in the direction of bringing Shakespeare to the screen through the text, or its equivalent in translation—Kozintsev, Peter Hall and Peter Brook among them.[5] In the end, Laurence Olivier is right; adapting the great theatre-scripts of Shakespeare to the screen is an artistic compromise, but one well worth making when the great performances of the plays are out of reach of most people who want to see them. The direct adaptation of Shakespeare, therefore, is a matter of overcoming the problem of compromise with the least possible loss to Shakespeare, on the one hand, and to the film itself on the other.

I give here an outline of the film:

A barren landscape is obscured by drifting mist. The camera turns in a slow pan to a chant which establishes the fatalism of the story to come—'Ambition destroys'. Slowly an isolated monolith becomes distinguishable through the mist; it indicates the site of what was once Cobweb Castle.

On a transitional dissolve, the castle of the past emerges out of the mist. A horseman rides furiously into the picture, menacing with fluttering pennants attached to his back. The pennants crackle in the wind like gunshot. The horseman leaps down, and beats with his fists on the door of the stronghold. Cut to—

The messenger on his knees before the Lord and his generals, sitting in line immobile. A second warrior-messenger enters in a state of collapse. A wailing kind of music, with vocal accompaniment, sounds behind the action. The Lord debates strategy with his generals.

A succession of new messengers arrives on horseback in turn; their chivalric helmets are decorated with plumes. This electrifying activity grows, both men and cameras on the move. Transition to—

A woodland landscape, saturated with rain. This is Cobweb Forest, 'where everyone loses his way'. The general Washizu (Macbeth) and his fellow-general Miki (Banquo) are lost. Washizu launches an arrow into the air. Hoarse laughter comes from the trees. They mount their horses and gallop away. Transition to—

A hut, its strange appearance enhanced by lighting. Does it hold some evil spirit? Washizu and Miki appear. A low chant is heard, eerie and monotonous; an old woman is spinning, lit by unearthly light. The chanting grows in its intensity, hoarse but insistent. The generals listen, transfixed; they hear the old woman proclaim, 'Life is like a flower that wilts. All men are mortal; there is only bondage where men fret, where there is lust and mortal greed. They must accept the judgment which spares neither sinner nor saint. They will vanish into nothingness.' The generals challenge the strange sexless creature, who then proclaims: 'Washizu will be Lord of Cobweb Castle, and Miki's sons rulers after him.' The old woman sits at her wheel, framed on either side by the warriors. Suddenly she vanishes, while mists drift about the men's feet. A mound of skulls and helmets ends the sequence. Cut to—

Washizu and Miki well advanced on their journey. Washizu: 'It was a strange dream.' They laugh it off. 'Both of us are in luck.' Transition to—

Thudding sounds as Washizu and Miki march, formal and helmeted, towards their Lord, who sits, thighs set wide apart, on his throne-seat. The Lord creates Washizu Master of the First Fort, fulfilling the first prophecy. Miki appears fat and benign, but Washizu is fierce and grimacing. Transition to—

A more lyrical mood, with lighter music. The scene is another stronghold, but one at peace: Washizu's home. A soldier is heard saying: 'This is a paradise after the Fort. Our Lord and Lady are happy.' Cut to—

Washizu striding about an almost bare room. Asaji (Lady Macbeth) sits on the floor, completely immobile. But she says, 'Have you made up your mind, my Lord?' He replies, 'We should not take our friends to task.' Still unmoving, she says, 'Kill, and take possession of Cobweb Castle. Our Lord once killed his Master and took possession of it.' It is a case of warrior against warrior. She sits, a Mona Lisa with her stillness and her enigmatic face, a decorative but deadly figure, isolated in the empty room furnished only by mats.

There is a sudden spate of action. Men run towards the camera, which travels back from them, as if avoiding the onrush. Men on horseback dash through long avenues of workers in the open fields; the workers wear great white circular hats. A procession of horses comes through the fields: the Lord of Cobweb Castle is arriving. A quick transition to—

Washizu and his lady, formally positioned. She sits as before on her mat in the right foreground. His booted feet and legs occupy the upper left of the picture. Asaji: 'Miki is his favourite.' Washizu demurs. Quick transition to—

A line of guards. It is revealed the Lord is to sleep in a 'forbidden room', which must be cleansed from the blood left from some previous murder. Cleaners come forward, carrying torches, and enter the forbidden room. Its walls are coated with dried blood. An owl hoots.

A decorative bed on a bare floor. Asaji's voice (off): 'The stage is set for you. Give the guards drugged wine.' The raven croaks. For the first time, Asaji's face becomes mobile, breaking into a grin: 'No man without ambition is a man,' she declares, and kneels before Washizu. Lights are seen moving behind the translucent walls as she stalks out, like a venomous doll.

With reverse lighting, she stalks into the area of the forbidden room. The camera tracks on to the prone figures of the drugged guards. Asaji returns to Washizu. He is seated, squatting on a mat set in front of a little metal screen. She creeps up on him and offers him a spear. He grasps it.

The moon. The owl hoots. Close shot of Washizu's savage, pent-up face. Tense, Asaji slowly seats herself on the mat, awaiting his return. Then she suddenly starts up to a crescendo of timpani beats and shrill whistles. Washizu returns. She seizes the spear from his bloodstained hands, takes it back to the scene of the murder and puts it in the hand of one of the drugged guards. She returns, fetches water, kneels, washes, dries her hands. Then she sees Washizu and rises. He is transfixed, unconscious of her. To a quick track of the camera, she runs and opens the gate, crying out, 'Murder!' Her cry brings Washizu back to consciousness. The drugged guards stagger to their feet, but Washizu sets on them with his sword. Cut to—

Crescendo of rushing men, their pennants fluttering and crackling in the sunlight. Horses' hooves. Panic. Cries of, 'Keep calm. Keep calm.' The Lord's sons, fearful, rush away. Asaji cries, 'Miki is guarding the Castle'.

Horsemen dash wildly through the misty woodlands to the Castle, the camera tracking with them very fast. The movement works to a powerful crescendo.

They are challenged at the gates of Cobweb Castle. Arrows fall down on them. Washizu decides to challenge Miki. But a message comes from Asaji—'His Lordship's coffin will secure the opening of the gates.' To thudding sounds, the Lord's coffin arrives, and is carried on men's shoulders into the castle. Washizu's eyes glint warily.

Washizu and Miki confront each other, and the funeral procession is led by them, as rival warriors. A cluster of weeping women bemoan the death of Miki's lady; it is suggested she committed suicide because she did not want to see an enemy take possession of Cobweb Castle. 'The evil spirit in the wood foresaw clearly,' says Miki. Transition to—

Washizu and Asaji as Lord and Lady of Cobweb Castle. Washizu is still defending Miki's loyalty against his wife's continued accusations. But, he says, we have no heir, whereas it is prophesied that Miki's sons will come to power. Asaji announces she is pregnant. Miki asserts that the prophecy concerning his son will come true.

Washizu's horse dashes madly round the compound. It cannot be caught, and runs wild.

Washizu and Asaji hold a feast. Sitting on their mats, they and their warrior guests listen while a band chants and mimes a song of treachery. There are two empty places. There is a slow building of climax as Washizu drinks. Finally, he lowers his saucer with equal slowness. Then he rises and falls back.

Miki, luminous and ghostly, appears momentarily in one of the empty places. Asaji, watching Washizu, laughs; 'He has drunk too much,' she says. And he echoes her: 'I am drunk.' But the vision of the ghost returns. Washizu, terrified, rushes to the place where the ghost sits, cutting at it with his sword. As the guests disperse in alarm and astonishment, Asaji mocks her husband.

A messenger, walking with precise and cat-like steps, brings Washizu Miki's head, wrapped in a cloth. But he says Miki's son has escaped. Washizu, enraged, strikes the messenger dead. Transition to—

A storm. The guards at the Castle mutter together. 'The rats are leaving the Castle.'

Washizu, alone. A woman approaches him timidly: 'The child was born dead.' Asaji is very ill. The woman wails as he strides away from her. Washizu starts to shout hysterically.

A messenger arrives with news of an impending attack on the Forts. There is a crescendo of movement among the warriors on horseback. The wind rages. The pennants flutter and crackle angrily. The thunder and the rain add to the confusion.

Washizu rushes from the Castle, crying out for the Evil One. He reaches the wood, and is greeted by mocking laughter. The lightning tears the sky. The weird woman is seen standing on a misty promontory. Washizu shouts: 'Will Miki's son succeed to the Castle?' The old woman replies: 'You will never lose a battle until Cobweb Forest is seen to move.' Then, to echoing laughter and voices, the succession of ghostly visions appears, one after the other, until Washizu is surrounded. Transition to—

An array of bannered troops lined up on open ground. They move forward and enter the forest. Cut to—

Inside Cobweb Castle, Washizu watches the circling enemy on the forest verge, looking down from the top of his battlements. He addresses his massed warriors in the compound of the Castle, and makes them roar with laughter at the prophecy that the forest might move. Transition to—

Night. Men are on the watch. There is a distant sound of the chopping of trees. Meanwhile, Washizu sits drinking with his officers.

There is a sudden movement of terror. A wild flock of ravens invades the Castle compound. Washizu claims this to be a lucky omen.

A mist falls. Sinister music. A group of weeping women fall

on their knees as Washizu approaches. He strides into his wife's room; she is hidden by a screen of hanging robes, which he pulls aside. Asaji is discovered feverishly laving her hands; her eyes are staring. She cannot keep her hands still. She is muttering, 'The smell of blood, the smell of blood.' At the sight of her, Washizu's movements become violently staccato. Transition to—

Panic among Washizu's warriors. 'The forest moves,' they cry. Washizu leaps to the upper rampart of the Castle, a wooden gallery surrounding the compound. He looks out.

A vast, waving forest of trees is moving towards the Castle through the mist. The branches animate weirdly as if they were living creatures.

Washizu orders his warriors back to their posts, but they begin to rain arrows on him. As the arrows cascade round him and enter his body, he goes mad, dashing hither and thither, transfixed by arrows. A final arrow pierces his throat. But still he lives, threatening his men, who retreat before him until he falls dead, lying in a pool of mist.

The film ends as it began, with the fateful chant. There is a slow dissolve to the monolith in the misty landscape where Cobweb Castle had once stood.

Notes to Chapter 9

1. Noh is an aristocratic art dating back to the fourteenth century, and reaching its height in the fifteenth and sixteenth centuries. It is a highly stylized form of drama with song and dance, played in masks, and achieving its height through the players' proficiency in speech and song (with specialized voice production and instrumental accompaniment) and choreographed movement. The situations in Noh plays turn on such basic human subjects as love, jealousy, revenge, filial piety and the spirit of *Samurai*, the fighting tradition of the warrior clans. The plays were originally composed by the performers themselves, and the Noh masks are decoratively stylized in form, character and facial expression.

Kabuki, on the other hand, is a later and more popularized form of choreographed, musical drama, dating back to the seventeenth century. The plots are more developed, and often more entertaining in their elaboration.

In both forms of drama men traditionally play the parts of women and achieve astonishing proficiency as female impersonators. A close relationship develops between the actors and those members of the audience who are knowledgeable of an art which represents a lifetime's dedicated application by star performers.

2. Tadao Sato most generously undertook to interview Kurosawa on my behalf, and the interview was first published in a special issue of the *Journal of the Society of Film and Television Arts* on 'Shakespeare and the Film'; I am the editor of this journal. I am grateful to Tadao Sato, author of a book on Kurosawa published in Japanese, for a number of details which appear in this chapter, and for the script extract.

3. *Ge-koku-jo* means that a retainer murders his lord and deprives him of his power. The age of civil wars, lasting for about one hundred years from the 1460s, is so named, and *ge-koku-jo* became characteristic of what happened in many areas of Japan.

4. The Noh songs refer to the epic poems used as scripts for the Noh plays.

5. 'Perhaps the most successful Shakespeare film ever made was the Japanese *Macbeth*, *Throne of Blood*. This had hardly any words, and none of them by Shakespeare.' Peter Hall in the *Sunday Times*, 26 January 1969.

10

Theatre into Film

MACBETH: THE WINTER'S TALE: OTHELLO: A MIDSUMMER NIGHT'S DREAM: HAMLET

The idea of filming stage productions, adapted in part for the screen, is as old as film history. It lay, as we have seen, at the root of the pioneer French *film d'art* and the Italian *film d'arte* movements, which attempted to bring an artificial dignity to films in the early years of the century, tempting, for example, members of the Comédie Française to record their stage performances in terms of violent gesticulation in silent films. The early films of Benson's *Richard III* and Forbes-Robertson's *Hamlet* were, in effect, records of stage productions. With the coming of sound, Bernard Shaw was among the first to try to insist on a word for word recording of his plays for the films; only much later did he come to realize that adaptation for the screen demanded far more radical changes than he had been prepared to allow initially.[1]

An obvious possibility in filming Shakespeare has always been to provide screen versions of established stars performing characters they have been accustomed to project from the stage. Apart from the Shakespearean films of Sir Laurence Olivier, this had not proved to be the case with the sound film until the 1960s, since by far the greater number of Shakespearean films made before that time tended to star players more experienced in the cinema than on the stage— many of them indeed appearing in Shakespeare if not actually for the first time, then certainly for the first time since the early stages of their careers before their days of stardom.

The 1960s brought a change. Shakespeare had been presented on television, frequently with considerable success, during the 1950s, and in the 1960s some outstanding presentations were televised which had been adapted from stage productions of note.[2] The success of Laurence Olivier's *Richard III* on American television did not, of course, pass unnoticed, and the increasing importance of the revenue to be obtained from the secondary presentations on television of Shakespearean films designed in the first place for release on big screen in the cinemas led to a number of productions of Shakespeare's plays as films.[3] George Schaefer's production of *Macbeth* in 1960, with Maurice Evans and Judith Anderson, was a film in its own right, but with Judith Anderson in particular in one of her established stage parts. During the later 1960s these Shakespearean film productions moved into a second phase, which was the adaptation to the screen of actual stage productions of note, made increasingly with international television in mind as well as the cinema.

George Schaefer's *Macbeth* was directed on a relatively modest scale. Shot in colour on location in the Scottish sunshine, or on the unpretentious castle sets designed by Edward Carrick (Edward Craig, the son of Gordon Craig), this film lacked any feeling for the haunted ferocity of Shakespeare's most fatalistic tragedy, and it should surely have been photographed in black and white. The film has, rather, the respectful earnestness of a routine, academic production in some conventional, well-established theatre. Judith Anderson's over-theatrical Lady Macbeth showed no recognition that to play this woman as a mere virago is to miss the whole point of her over-strained and essentially feminine nature, which leads to her eventual collapse. Maurice Evans's blusteringly masculine Macbeth reveals nothing of the flawed conscience and inner weakness of this man, which make him lose his nerve when driven by his wife to commit the one murder most necessary to the fulfilment of their ambitions, though he is only too ready to consolidate his power, once he has achieved it, by using agents to commit his further crimes for him. It is a major miscalculation in the film to let Macbeth merely dream of his final, and fatal, encounter with the witches instead of facing them out of sheer necessity. Reliance on the occult is an essential part of Macbeth's weakness, and his ever-increasing commitment to witchcraft central to the play's theme. Macbeth's bombast is mere noise to cover over his secret fears and his growing realization that 'naught's had, all's spent', a fatalism which finally overcomes him.

Macbeth is one of Shakespeare's more difficult plays; its proper interpretation on the stage has been the subject of debate by actors and actresses at least since the eighteenth century, and turns, among other things, on the changing relationship, and balance of power, between Macbeth and his wife. The over traditional performances played on one note by Maurice Evans and Judith Anderson ineffectually mask the great opportunities which the sheer closeness of the film to both character and action makes possible. This relationship scarcely exists in Orson Welles's film owing to the weakness in the playing of Lady Macbeth, the concentration by Orson Welles on the brooding power of his own performance and on the fulfilment of the theme of the play as he sees it—the defeat of evil paganism by a resurgent Christianity. Only in Kurosawa's remarkable transmutation of the play to medieval Japan is the extraordinary relationship of Macbeth and his wife realized, though in highly stylized performances. A fully realized film of *Macbeth* in its original language has yet to be made; perhaps as I write, by Roman Polanski.

More recently, in the case of Shakespearean films, we have gone back on ourselves; theatre productions have been turned into films with the minimum of adaptation, largely for screening on television. This was specially true in Britain, where in any case there has been a long-established tradition of filming successful modern plays, though with script adaptation—for example, *Look Back in Anger*, *A Taste of Honey*, *The Entertainer*, and, on a more experimental basis, *The Caretaker*. But it was not until the mid 1960s that a series of British stage productions of Shakespeare was filmed.[4] Among the first was Frank Dunlop's so-called 'Pop Theatre' production of *The Winter's Tale* for the Edinburgh Festival in 1966. Produced by the Canadian, Peter Snell, and featuring Laurence Harvey (Leontes), Jane Asher (Perdita), and Moira Redmond (Hermione), it played 151 minutes. Photographed in somewhat crude Eastmancolour and acted without distinction, the film did little to inspire confidence in this utility form of film-making, which could only be justified if it resulted in a clear and true record of a really distinguished stage production. This version of *The Winter's Tale* suffered badly from over-emphasis both in the acting and in the continuous, non-selective use of close-up— this obviously done in order to anticipate the needs of television.

It was the year before, in 1965, that the most notable of these theatrical film-records had appeared. This was a Technicolor, Panavision production of *Othello*, with Laurence Olivier as the Moor, directed by Stuart Burge and based on John Dexter's quatercentenary production for the National Theatre of Great Britain. The production company responsible for the film, BHE (British Home Entertainments), headed by Anthony Havelock-Allan and Lord Brabourne, in addition to sponsoring Joseph Losey's *King and Country*, had already begun to specialize in the production of theatrical recordings of stage successes for television, including Laurence Olivier's own production for the National Theatre of *Uncle Vanya*.

The *réclame* of Olivier's interpretation of Othello as a Negro has exceeded anything experienced in the British theatre since the war, and was approached only by the acclamation for Paul Scofield's Lear in Peter Brook's production for the Royal Shakespeare Company in Stratford and London during 1962, which had to wait almost a decade before it, too, was filmed. Olivier's interpretation became the subject of a book by Kenneth Tynan—*Othello* (1966).

The aim of the film, which was specially shot under studio conditions, was, in the words of the producer, 'to recreate completely the atmosphere, effect and immediacy of the theatre performance, using the basis of film technique'. Anthony Havelock-Allan said:

> We considered it important to preserve and enhance this *Othello* and more or less present it as one might have seen it at the National Theatre.
> After all, the whole object was to capture the absolute magic of the theatre on this occasion.
> We have put the best cinema resources at the service of great theatre, and will thus enable millions of people throughout the world, who would not have had the remotest chance of seeing Sir Laurence on the stage, to share the experience.

Nothing was cut from the stage version, and the film runs for two hours fifty minutes. Three widescreen Panavision cameras recorded the long speeches simultaneously, so that they could be spoken without interruption, and the different shots used for editing. The stylized studio sets designed for the film by William Kellner were deliberately based on Jocelyn Herbert's stage sets, and as far as possible the players were enabled to recreate in the studio their stage performances as little disturbed by the cameras as possible. There were no exterior shots, no special effects, only straight, not very pleasing colour photography, using a variety of set-ups. Stuart Burge had had a distinguished career, both as a theatre and television director, but his only film experience as such had been his previous recording of *Uncle Vanya* for BHE. The resources of the cinema are used with almost painstaking restraint, especially for a film of this length—for example, the overhead shot when Othello falls in a fit comes as a visual shock.

The effect of the film on big screen is often excessive, the camera being too near for ease either of observation or hearing. It is like being on the stage itself, with the cast; one is frequently over-conscious of the sheer theatrical projection necessary in the theatre. The only principal character who scores from this recording is Frank Finlay, whose deliberately quiet, prosaic NCO-type Iago, jealous of Cassio's promotion, matches the close-shots precisely, and tunes with Robert Lang's beautifully muted performance as Roderigo.

This is not the place to argue the nature of the interpretations—whether or not this is the right Iago, or even the right Othello—*was* Shakespeare's conception of the Moor an African Negro? In an interview for *Life* magazine, Olivier spoke of 'that color difference—the whole play seeps through with it . . . It's tremendously, highly sexual . . . I'm sure Shakespeare meant there to be a great splash of shock'. He complains that Shakespeare introduces far too many climaxes in the part, forcing the actor to play too often near the top of his range—'all beckoning you to scream your utmost'. On the other hand, he says:

> In Shakespeare I always try to reassure the audience initially that they are not going to see some grotesque, outsized dimension of something which they can't understand or sympathize with. If you have succeeded in the initial moments, either by a very strong stamp of characterisation so they recognise you as a real guy, or by a quiet approach—then I think there's no end

to where you can lead them in size of acting. God knows, you have to be enormously big as Othello.

Then he adds:

On the other hand, self-indulgence—getting carried away—is such a very great, common pitfall for an actor. You must always be like a jockey on a racehorse—watching, watching, watchful, watch it—listening all the time to one's self.

This is true, but the problem in this *Othello* is that the watchfulness, the calculation of the performance, sometimes shows. It probably would not have done so had the performance been conceived in the first place for closeness of observation by the cameras. Othello is a supremely difficult if not impossible part to render successfully except from the distance of the stage for which it was specifically written. Nevertheless, one is more than grateful to have this record of a performance which must rank as one of the great bravura achievements of the century in the British theatre.

Certain new incentives behind the filming of contemporary productions of Shakespeare have been described for me by Lord Birkett,[5] the producer of the next film to be considered, Peter Hall's version of *A Midsummer Night's Dream*, for Royal Shakespeare Enterprises, which had its première on American television in February 1969.

Ten years ago, if you made a Shakespeare film, the play you chose was automatically regarded as taboo to others because it was a classic-which-had-been-filmed-already. Nowadays, not only is there a grave danger of the whole canon being filmed before long, but several versions of the more popular plays are appearing. *Hamlet* has been filmed by Olivier and by Kozintzev; Tony Richardson has just done a version with Nicol Williamson, Richard Harris is reputed to be planning one, and Burton's Broadway performance was run in cinemas on a sort of closed-circuit-replay of a tape, for two performances only. Here already are a number of rival versions of one classic. Producers of Shakespeare films used to console themselves that even if their films didn't earn much money at the time, they would somehow become rich in their old age. Being 'classics', these films were bound to be shown somewhere every year and would continue to earn small residuals for ever. Nowadays, it's likely to be only the most recent film version which is played, and older versions may become out of date—or rarely shown.

There will, of course, always be a value in comparison. Even so, the exclusivity that a film-maker used to have over a Shakespeare subject is a thing of the past.

As for the deal-making, financial, aspects of Shakespearean films, there's no doubt that television has made a great deal of difference. Films are regularly financed today by including the eventual television residuals in the deal (that is, pre-selling the film for three years' time to a television company and using the money you get as part of the budget); also, several films have been made for showing first on television and thereafter in cinemas. The usual pattern of distribution (achieve a reputation in the cinemas, then sell to TV) is not necessarily the only pattern. It may be possible to show a film *first* on television, achieving a considerable amount of publicity and a very wide audience, and *then* show it in cinemas so that those who missed it, those who want to see it again, and those who merely heard about it, can go and add to the revenue. This scheme has only arisen because of 'the classics'; obviously it would not apply to a normal feature film. The feeling is that a film of Shakespeare will not date; the sheer newness of the film is not as big a commercial factor as usual.

Peter Hall developed this point, before discussing the film as a whole, in a published conversation he had with me in the summer of 1969, which we titled, 'On the Dank and Dirty Ground':

R.M.: A great many people seem to be engaged in making Shakespearean films at present. To what extent do you think television has any influence on this?

P.H.: I think people wholly connected with movies tend to get stuffy about television, as if it were automatically inferior. I think the future is more exciting for us all because of television—films will become more flexible, more varied because of it, let alone the possibilities that lie ahead in the cassette film and the EVR system. Soon we shall be involved in creating visual long-playing records; we shall be filming opera, Shakespeare, the classics of the theatre. And it will certainly not be enough to record a good stage performance direct on film. The films must be new productions in their own right.

R.M.: You believe, then, that there must be a new conception, technically, before successful stage productions are brought to the screen?

P.H.: Yes, of course. Film is a different language. At the moment I'm obsessed with the problems of presenting opera on the screen. This raises the issue of the physical closeness of the singer to the audience, something alien to the opera.

R.M.: But how can you dodge this special element, the need to project outwards in a big way what was originally created precisely to be projected in great opera houses?

P.H.: I think works tend to be over-projected in theatres. We confuse energy and meaning. I don't like excessive projection, especially for Shakespeare. In opera and Shakespeare, 'projection' is often a physical disguise of lack of true feeling. I like things to be kept cool, flexible, 'witty' in the eighteenth century sense of the word. I like the drama in the clash of ideas rather than noise. I made the *Dream* in close shot not because of lack of money, or because it was likely to be shown on television. I wanted it close shot because this seems to me the only way to scrutinise coolly the marked ambiguity of the text, and the cinema can do this better than the theatre. In an excess of enthusiasm I probably shot the film ten per cent too much in close up; the sheer concentration proves rather wearing. But in opera—! Well, this kind of treatment just couldn't work. Opera's essentially rhetorical, though true. Most of the time Shakespeare's just the opposite, anti-rhetorical, speaking very tight to his audience. Rhetorical declaiming of Shakespeare becomes just an exciting noise, without meaning. Shakespeare had to deal with close-packed theatres, a huge audience compressed in a small space and stationed all round the actors, really on top of them. And he wrote so that the actors could talk literally to them, not boom away over their heads.

R.M.: This raises the whole business of handling speech from the screen. What are the differences between, say, speaking Shakespeare at Stratford and on film?

P.H.: In the way I've worked on Shakespeare, it differs very little. I distrust any kind of 'projection' until you're quite sure you know what it is you need to project. The greatest influence on me, on my generation, was Leavis, who believed above everything in a critical examination of the text, the search for meaning and metaphor. If you boom Shakespeare you lose him. You end up with vocal varnish. It's true there are areas in Shakespeare when mere rhetoric does occur, and then indulgence of this sort is necessary. And there is deliberate rhetoric like the Player King. But in his case, of course, Shakespeare is showing up the kind of rhetoric he believed to be out of date in the theatre, his theatre. The trouble is that the theatre in the nineteenth century went in for rhetoric, the set-piece recitation. I believe in the other school of acting, that of powerful restraint—what Anna Magnani, for example, was doing here the other week in *La Lupa*. Or what Duse, one imagines from the accounts of her and her film clips, must have done as distinct from Bernhardt. So when one is filming, the closeness of the camera is no embarrassment. It is, in fact, a support. It insists on thoughtful speech! My company working in the *Dream* already appreciated this because of the work they had done with me in the theatre. All we had to do was make sure the faces did nothing excessive in expression during the close shots. I deliberately chose to use post-synch.; this gave me the opportunity to speak with lightness and precision. We enjoyed this stage of the work, though it took months to do. In any case, shooting out of doors means shooting in a terribly noisy world. I thought an open-air acoustic would be wrong for the *Dream*. It's an artificial play, not a natural one requiring natural sound.

R.M.: Why use a location, then, and not keep the whole thing in the studio?

P.H.: Because a studio could have betrayed us into the wrong kind of theatricality. And this, understand me, is dangerous for something which is already in itself theatrical. To film Shakespeare out of doors enables one to select what one wants from nature, from actuality. You don't want a total, out-door reality. Selectivity comes through the camera itself, which renders nature in artificial terms to just the right degree. In a studio, what you would achieve is a selection of something which is in itself a selection created by the art director. You see, what I would like to do is film an opera out of doors. The camera-image of necessity would modify the actuality it saw. In the studio you would get the opposite effect; it's a semblance of actuality which the camera then stylizes still further. On the other hand, in the theatre no one really expects actuality. If I were to do the *Dream* on the stage again, I would just have a large circle of green carpet to represent the wood. And a marble floor for the palace. The fairies would bring in the carpet themselves, and so create the wood when we wanted it. Lighting and the words would do the rest. But to try to achieve this kind of effect with a movie camera would be idiotic. For the camera, the carpet would just be a real, green carpet. What the camera sees is always taken to be real, however much, through photography, this actuality becomes stylized.

R.M.: How does Kozintsev fit in here, using in his *Hamlet* a castle ruin as location, trimmed with additional, artificial structures?

P.H.: I don't quarrel with Kozintsev for his use of reality in his images. He used a real castle, and his art director manufactured some further, imitation reality for him. If anything, there was too much reality. There was more castle than was needed.

I've tried in the *Dream* to get away completely from the expected Shakespearean setting, which is essentially nineteenth century and Pre-Raphaelite. The kind of approach associated with Mendelssohn's incidental music. That's how the *Dream* has always been presented, culminating in Reinhardt's stage productions, and his film of the 1930s. None of these people could have really looked at the text. Or if they did, they chose deliberately to disregard it. The *Dream* is quite clearly a play about an English summer in which the seasons have gone wrong. It is winter when it should be summer; everywhere is wet and muddy. This is described by Titania in a central speech. This is why I shot much of the film in the rain, during a bad-weather period lasting about six weeks. Titania's speech explaining this has often been cut in the past, yet it is the essence of the situation. The King and Queen of the Fairies, embodying animal nature, are quarrelling, and their quarrels have upset the balance of nature. This is what the play is all about. It is not a pretty, balletic affair, but erotic, physical, down to earth. All this, but with great charm and humour as well. Whether the critics liked it or not. I'm glad to say I got an extraordinary number of letters, mostly from young people on both sides of the Atlantic, supporting this interpretation.

R.M.: Did Kott's interpretation of the play as an essentially dark one have any influence?

P.H.: Certainly. Kott's understanding of the ambivalence of Shakespeare has been as useful to us as Leavis's insistence of scrutinising the text for its real meaning. But Kott isn't everything. He lacks, for example, any real understanding of Shakespeare's humour. He overweights his interpretation. He thinks the plays are neurotic.

R.M.: But politically he's important. For the historical plays.

P.H.: Marvellous. I read him for the first time in a proof copy when travelling to Stratford for the initial rehearsals of the three *Henrys*. It was like a revelation to have what I was going to try to do confirmed quite independently by this scholar in Poland.

R.M.: Have you any special approach to editing Shakespearean films as a result of making the *Dream*? Mankiewicz, for example, almost entirely eliminated the reaction shot in his *Julius Caesar*, in order to concentrate all the time on the speakers.

P.H.: I believe in editing to the rhythm of the text. Most Shakespearean films, those using the English text, drive me mad because the visual rhythm contradicts the verbal. The verbal rhythm derives, of course, from Shakespeare's use of beat in verse. The important thing in Shakespeare, as in a Mozart aria, is phrasing. There must be some awareness of the end of the line even in Shakespeare's mature verse with its run-on lines; the end of the line still needs marking. Actors tend to meet this requirement in different ways—Peggy Ashcroft, for example, hits the last word in the line percussively; John Gielgud elongates it. But everyone has to do something. The modern generation from the acting schools, I've found, have never even heard of the iambic pentameter. But it's the basic unit of Shakespearean phrasing. Shakespeare has all the formal strength of the great French dramatists, without their rigidity. So the speaking of Shakespeare must conform to this rhythmic pattern. But the traditional Shakespeare film in English has ignored any kind of reflection of the aural pattern in the visual pattern. They should surely match. In the *Dream* my aim was to create a picture rhythm by cutting to the verbal pattern—that is, on the caesura, or at the end of the line.

R.M.: Is there anything to be learnt from Kozintsev's work, for example, or Kurosawa's in their Shakespearean adaptations?

P.H.: Their case was different, of course, because they didn't have to use Shakespeare's text. I think if you make a film from Shakespeare you must do one of two things. The first is throw away the text altogether, as you have to do in the case of a translation, and develop the fable with all its atmosphere. This is what happens in *Throne of Blood* and the Russian *Hamlet*. Alternatively, you work with the text. Then you must cut the text first, and make the camera support its close interpretation. To make an absolutely conventional film, with a fully developed film technique, is impossible in the case of Shakespeare, since too much normal film art contradicts the technique of the plays, at least as far as their most important element, the text, is concerned. But the medium of film can certainly be used to communicate the text most effectively, even to the extent of making its meaning clearer than is sometimes possible in the theatre. After all, in the film of the *Dream* we cut virtually nothing from the text. We used exactly the same text as we did at Stratford, and yet we managed to bring the film in eight minutes shorter than the running time of the stage production.

In an article written earlier for the *Sunday Times* (26 January 1969), Peter Hall emphasized certain of these points about Shakespeare:

> It's true that Shakespeare's structural rhythms, the counterpoint between scenes, often work in the same way as good film editing. But, in a more important respect, Shakespeare is no screen writer. He is a verbal dramatist, relying on the associative and metaphorical power of words. Action is secondary. What is meant, is said. Even his stage action is verbalised before or after the event.
> This is bad screen writing. A good film-script relies on contrasting visual images. What is spoken is of secondary importance. And so potent is the camera in convincing us that we are peering at reality, that dialogue is best under-written or elliptical. . . .

The verbal essence of Shakespeare is inescapably non-cinematic. In spite of this—indeed, in contradiction to it—I have tended to use the advantages of the cinema not to make a film in the accepted sense, but to communicate his words. . . .

But the film is not intended as a reproduction of a stage presentation. The emphases and the visual style are completely different. We shot the whole film on location. The place had to look *actual*, like the actors. Fairy tales must be concrete if they are to be human and not whimsical.

Shakespeare's play is set in Athens. But this classical device is to distance and romanticise what is, in fact, a very Elizabethan and very English play. Bottom and his mates are the workers of Warwickshire. Theseus is no pagan warrior, but a country Duke who practises an essentially English brand of pragmatism when things get difficult. The Renaissance conceits of the four lovers belong to the Elizabethan love-lyrics. And the fairies in their wilfulness and sexiness are not classical, but sprites of Hallowe'en.

The play is earthy and passionate, about Beauty and the Beast and the anguish of young love. Its world is Northern rather than Mediterranean. . . .

We shot our film at the end of September and the weather conditions were ideal: rain, frost and mist. The unit suffered hell, especially the naked fairies.

Our setting was Compton Verney in Warwickshire, a classical house of the seventeenth century with a simplicity that avoids the grandiloquent. It had outlying buildings for the Athenian workers, a chapel, an obelisk, a lake, and, most important, a tangled wood.

We did long takes, shooting quickly, so the actors could sustain their feelings and preserve continuity. Shakespeare works in paragraphs of emotion rather than sentences. The whole film was photographed by a hand-held camera, kept as steady as possible. The slight movement gave life to the formal text, and of course, great manœuvrability. . . .

This is not a film *from* a stage production or a film *based* on the play. It attempts to bend the medium of film to reveal the full quality of the text. In the precise sense of the word, it therefore may not be a film at all.

Peter Hall had directed *A Midsummer Night's Dream* three times in nine years for the Royal Shakespeare Company, and his cast for the film derived from these productions. It received a disastrous press; the critics, as one might expect, were looking for the wrong kind of magic—the magic of Mendelssohn (that fatal, over-romantic influence from the nineteenth century), rather than the earthy, elvish, spiteful magic of Shakespeare's play, with its erotic mischief and dark comedy played in one of those out-of-sorts and thoroughly wet summers to which England was only too prone in Shakespeare's day as it is in our own.

The film can only appeal to those ready to accept this entirely different approach to the play. Peter Suschitzky's colour photography emphasizes the fairies' lead-green, earthen colour. They appear to be covered with cobwebs. Certain simple cinematic devices are used—the quarrels of Titania and Oberon are dispersed in time and place as they move magically about the woods; Puck flashes into vision with the crack of a whip; Oberon appears and disappears at will when he administers his supernatural aphrodisiacs; there is even a subliminal touch about the first appearance of Bottom with his ass's head. The lovers are gormless, mixed-up adolescents, the worker-players earnest fools, while the nobles behave like English squirearchy. There could not be a greater contrast between this version of the play and that of Reinhardt, made over thirty years earlier and reflecting the romantic, spectacular tradition of nineteenth-century Shakespearean production at its height.

Tony Richardson's most interesting experiment in both staging and filming *Hamlet* in the Round House theatre in London during 1969 came as a result of an attempt, as Richardson put it, to 'free the theatre from the tyranny of the proscenium arch and the social habits which go with it'.[6] The Round House is a vast Victorian structure built over a century ago; originally a shed for locomotive repairs, it became a warehouse. More recently it was converted into an open, popular theatre for Arnold Wesker's Centre 42 arts project, by arrangement with which Tony Richardson produced *Hamlet*, starring Nicol Williamson as the Prince and Marianne Faithfull as Ophelia. The idea of filming the production was present from the start.

Richardson regards the Round House as

a masterpiece of Victorian architecture which will put the actors into immediate contact with the audience instead of being stuck behind the picture-frame of a proscenium. It does away with that terrible formality, and lets actors speak in a room instead of up on an artificial platform . . . The most vital thing is space, and at the Round House we have that. . . . Originally it was a building for fixing trains, and I still want it to be a magical engineering shed, but for the theatre. . . .

And with regard to the film: 'Another example of the flexibility of the Round House—we shall simply move cameras in during the daytime, though it will be a real film, not a photographed version of the stage production.'

The film in fact was shot as a low-budget venture by Richardson's company, Woodfall, using the same cast, but elaborating the spatial movement of the production by using, for example, the cellars at the Round House and parts of the surrounding district as well as the stage itself. This ascetic production remained, however, essentially the same in treatment and spirit as it was in the live theatre.

It is played in the shadows of the brick-built labyrinth of the Roundhouse, looking like the remoter caverns of a vast, deserted warehouse. A brick wall affords a background to the opening title, and the watchers on the ramparts are seen against this same plain setting—the camera turning, twisting, and travelling in close shot to follow their movements and catch their faces. Suddenly they become transfixed with fear as the Ghost appears, never to be seen as a presence but manifest only as a voice accompanied by a brilliant light revealing the blenched horror on the observers' faces. The text of the scene is cut back to the barest essentials, in order to emphasize the impact made by the Ghost, whose appearance is accompanied by gong-like reverberations.

Horatio, as played by Gordon Jackson, is in effect a bespectacled and middle-aged don. As the friend and 'fellow-student' of Hamlet in Wittenburg University, he prepares us for a mature interpretation of the Prince, which implies the advanced nature of Hamlet's academic standing; Jan Kott, after all, would have us see Hamlet as a man primarily dedicated to university life. Whether Kott exaggerates this position or not, Hamlet is obviously no adolescent student, but a man well on into his twenties, a post-graduate scholar. The Hamlet of Nicol Williamson is just such a man, an academic summoned back home for his mother's marriage and prevented from returning to his studies by the sudden intrusion into his life of the mission he is so

OTHELLO (Morocco 1952). Director, Orson Welles

Othello (Orson Welles) with Iago (Micheál MacLiammóir)

Iago with Roderigo (Robert Coote)

Othello and Desdemona (Suzanne Cloutier)

Othello and Desdemona

Othello after the murder
of his wife

CHIMES AT MIDNIGHT
(Spain-Switzerland 1965).
Director, Orson Welles

Falstaff (Orson Welles) and
Mistress Quickly (Margaret
Rutherford)

Falstaff, Mistress Quickly and
Doll Tearsheet (Jeanne
Moreau)

Prince Hal and his
father, Henry IV
(Keith Baxter and
John Gielgud)

Falstaff

OTHELLO (U.S.S.R. 1955).
Director, Sergei Yutkevitch

Othello (Sergei Bondarchuk)
and Desdemona (Irina
Skobtseva)

Othello and Iago (Andrei
Popov)

OTHELLO

Othello

Othello and Iago

HAMLET (U.S.S.R.
1964). Director,
Grigori Kozintsev

Claudius (Michail
Nazwanov) and
Gertrude (Eliza
Radzin-Szolkonis)

Hamlet (Innokenti
Smoktunovsky)
and Gertrude

Hamlet and the
musicians

Ophelia (Anasta
Vertinskaya) lea
deportment

Hamlet and
Ophelia

Hamlet and
Ophelia

Ophelia in madness

Ophelia and Laertes (O. Oleksenko)

Hamlet and the Gravedigger (V. Kolpakor)

KING LEAR
(U.S.S.R. 1970).
Director, Grigori
Kozintsev

Lear (Yuri Yarvet)

Goneril (Elza
Radzin), Regan
(Galina Volchek),
and Cordelia
(Valentina
Chendrikova)

Lear and Goneril

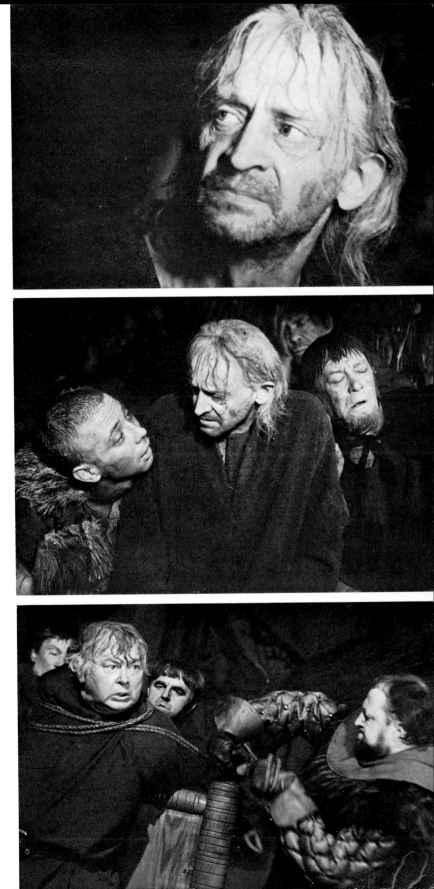

Lear in destitution

Lear with the Fool
(Oleg Dal) and
Kent (Vladimir
Emelianov)

Gloucester (Karl
Sebris) bound by
the Duke of
Cornwall

Gloucester and Edgar (Leonard Merzin)

Edgar, Gloucester and Lear

Lear and Cordelia

JULIUS CAESAR
(U.S.A. 1953).
Director, Joseph
L. Mankiewicz

Caesar (Louis
Calhern) on his
way to the Games

Casca (Edmond
O'Brien) and
Cassius (John
Gielgud)

Casca delivers the
first blow against
Caesar

Brutus (James Mason) addresses the Roman crowds

Antony (Marlon Brando)

Brutus in his tent

JULIUS CAESAR
Great Britain
(1969). Director,
Stuart Burge

The murder of
Caesar (John
Gielgud)

Antony (Charlton
Heston) addresses
the Roman crowds

Antony leads his
armies

ROMEO AND JULIET (Great Britain-Italy 1954). Director, Renato Castellani

Mercutio (Aldo Zello) attacks Tybalt (Enzo Fiermonte) outside the Capulet Palace

Benvolio (Bill Travers) urges Romeo (Laurence Harvey) to flee Verona; Tybalt's body lies on the steps

The body of Mercutio is carried away

ROMEO AND
JULIET

Juliet (Susan
Shentall) with
her maids

Juliet with Friar
Laurence
(Mervyn Johns)

The Nurse
(Flora Robson)
discovers Juliet
unconscious

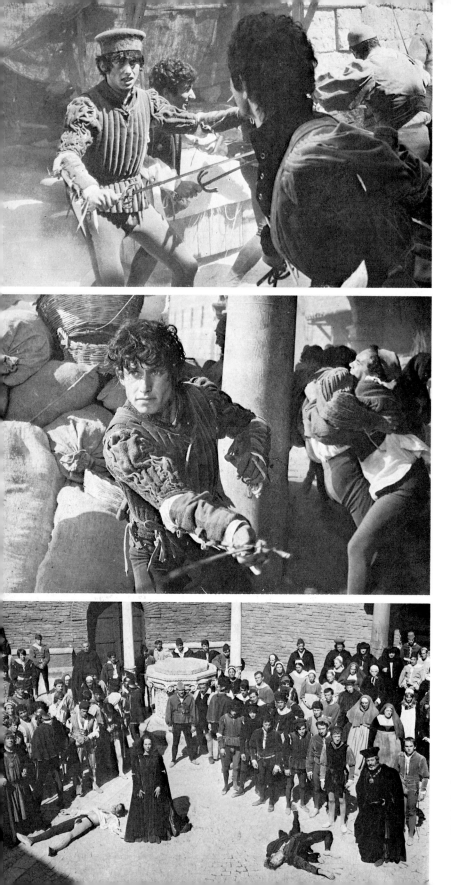

ROMEO AND
JULIET (Great
Britain-Italy
1968). Director,
Franco
Zeffirelli

Tybalt (Michael
York) faces
Benvolio (Bruce
Robinson)

Tybalt

The bodies of
Tybalt and
Mercutio after
the fight

Juliet (Olivia Hussey)

Romeo (Leonard
Whiting)

Romeo and Juliet

THE TAMING OF
THE SHREW
(U.S.A.-Italy 196
Director, Franco
Zeffirelli

Katharina
(Elizabeth Taylor

Baptista (Michael
Hordern) and his
daughter Bianca
(Natasha Pyne)

Petruchio
(Richard Burton)

THE WINTER'S TALE (Great
Britain 1966). Director, Frank
Dunlop

Leontes (Laurence Harvey)

Hermione (Moira Redmond)

OTHELLO (Great Britain 1965). Director, Stuart Burge

Othello (Laurence Olivier) and Desdemona (Maggie Smith)

Iago (Frank Finlay) and Roderigo (Robert Lang)

The fight between Cassio (Derek Jacobi) and Montano (Edward Hardwicke)

Othello and
Desdemona

Desdemona

Othello and
Desdemona

HAMLET (Great Britain 1969). Director, Tony Richardson

Hamlet (Nicol Williamson) and Polonius (Mark Dignam)

Hamlet and his mother, Gertrude (Judy Parfitt)

ill-fitted to carry out—the avenging of his father's murder by exposing and assassinating the new King, his mother's second husband. Nicol Williamson's Hamlet is clipped of speech and thin of voice—nervous, energetic, intellectual; resentful of the role which destiny has imposed on him. He is the misfit at the Danish court, both as a Prince and as a son.

The Court in which Hamlet is trapped is a barbaric community steeped in alcohol—Anthony Hopkins's Claudius is a 'bloat' rather than a lascivious King, and lacks the stature or authority of the autocrat which is given Claudius by Basil Sydney in Olivier's *Hamlet* or by Michail Nazwanov in Kozintsev's film. Again the camera twists about in close-shot until it finally rests on Hamlet. The first soliloquy ('O, that this too too solid flesh would melt—') is spoken slightly off-camera, with no pretension of being voiced thought. Williamson's speech is quick, intense, nasal; he shakes with anger over his mother's re-marriage. The pitch of this, and of the interchange which follows with Horatio, is naturalistic, even deliberately prosaic—the relationship is close and immediate, on the level of 'real' life rather than on the more elevated plane of poetry. At the mention of the Ghost, Hamlet's eyes dart about in nervous paroxysm; his breathing becomes hard, his utterance low and quick with growing anxiety. Then the film cuts sharply to a very pale Ophelia and a wanton Laertes; rather perversely, they seem to enjoy an incestuous relationship; she laughs knowingly at her brother's mention of her 'chaste treasure'. Later, her relationship with Hamlet is at least suggested as having been sexual, and in consequence she is the more upset at his fierce rejection of her.

Hamlet's encounter with the Ghost is over-consciously embellished with sound effects which lessen the tension of his horrified reaction—in contrast with his whispered speech, there is a gong-like reverberation and an echoing of key words from the Ghost's voice ('lov'd'; 'murder'; 'Queen'; 'incest'; 'remember me') which become technically over-emphasized. Hamlet's distraction is reflected by jerkiness of speech and staccato breathing; his curious tricks of pronunciation become accentuated ('tew' for 'too'; 'yew' for 'you'); finally he collapses in the arms of his anxious friends. 'To be or not to be' is spoken lying in bed, his head turning in close-shot to speak directly to the audience; his character is further revealed through the cynical way in which he refers to 'conscience' making cowards of us all, and he chuckles almost maliciously on the words, 'lose the name of action'. He finds Ophelia swinging in a hammock; he mocks her, even kissing her when she says she was 'the more deceived' by his former advances. The camera finally pulls back to reveal Polonius spying on the scene.

The scene with Rosencrantz and Guildenstern is played with equally cynical attack—'Were you not sent for?' In his affected madness with Polonius, Hamlet's voice rises almost to a squeak; in the Queen's closet, after the light of the Ghost's intervention has lit Hamlet's face (but not the Queen's), his voice becomes broken with sobs, and the lines, 'But go not to my uncle's bed' and 'I'll blessing beg of you', involve him in a complete emotional breakdown. These tears seem forced, and somehow frustrate the real emotion of this scene. Hamlet's cynical mood returns when he kisses the King on the words, 'Farewell, dear mother'. The scene when Hamlet refrains from killing the King at prayer is omitted, though part of the prayer itself is retained—ineffectively, as always. The King's momentary, isolated act of compunction never seems to ring true.

In the final scenes much use is made of Hamlet's and Horatio's profiles in close two-shot. At the end of the film (the last line is Horatio's—'And flights of angels sing thee to thy rest'), Horatio's profile is set up horizontally directly over the profile of the dead Hamlet, which, left alone on the screen, acts as background to the final credits, which are spoken. The whole of the film emphasizes closeness of observation and the mobility of the camera—even the duel scene is shot close-in, with candle flames breaking the foreground as the camera swivels to keep the duellists in vision. And accompanying this closeness is the essentially ascetic treatment of the characters—the King and Queen rather underplayed, Ophelia uncertainly placed between lasciviousness and innocence, Polonius a quiet spoken, conspiratorial diplomat without conscience. Hamlet himself remains throughout the neurotic outsider, a nervous academic far removed from the romantic, melancholy Prince of the past. This is a Hamlet with contemporary psychology uppermost, by-passing both the unvenomed poetry and the dynamic grandeur of Shakespeare's tragic protagonist.

130

1. See Donald P. Costello, *The Serpent's Eye: Shaw and the Cinema* (University of Notre Dame Press (Indiana), 1966), and the initial review of the book, giving further facts, in *The Times Literary Supplement*, 19 October 1966.

2. The chief studio productions of Shakespeare's plays in Britain by B.B.C. Television during the 1940s and earlier 1950s included Ian Atkins's *As You Like It* (1946), Michael Barry's *Romeo and Juliet* (1947), George More O'Ferrall's *Hamlet* (1947), *Macbeth* (1949) and *Othello* (1950), Royston Morley's *King Lear* (1948), *Richard II* (1950) and *Henry V* (1951), Desmond Davis's *The Merchant of Venice* (1949), Harold Clayton's *Twelfth Night* (1950) and Stephen Harrison's *Julius Caesar* (1951) and *King John* (1952). Two B.B.C. repertory series appeared in the 1960s—Peter Dews's *An Age of Kings*, serializing during 1951 in fifteen fortnightly one-hour plays the essential action of *Richard II*, *Henry IV* i and ii, *Henry V*, *Henry VI* i, ii and iii, and *Richard III*; and *The Spread of the Eagle*, serializing during 1963 in nine one-hour plays *Coriolanus*, *Julius Caesar* and *Antony and Cleopatra*. Another notable production in the quatercentenary year, 1964, was a large-scale recorded production of *Hamlet*, with Christopher Plummer, made by Philip Saville on location at Kronborg Castle in Denmark. During 1964–5 Michael Barry produced, and Michael Hayes and Robin Midgley directed, the celebrated three-part adaptation of Shakespeare's *Henry VI* i, ii and iii and *Richard III* known collectively as *The Wars of the Roses*, and made by Peter Hall and John Barton for production by the Royal Shakespeare Company at Stratford-upon-Avon. On television the series was presented in April 1965 in three three-hour parts, featuring Peggy Ashcroft, David Warner, Roy Dotrice, Ian Holm and Donald Sinden.

3. Laurence Olivier writes about this presentation of *Richard III* on American television: 'I think the temptation behind this deal, which was made by Robert Dowling and which I must say was very strongly deplored by me, was that by obtaining whatever the figure was from television he would have already achieved the equivalent of the first million dollars at the box office. This idea was too heady a one to resist, I suppose, and there it was. But in my opinion it did the film great damage. It was shot in VistaVision using a marvellous colour palette by Roger Furse, but the grandeur and the clever effects were of course completely lost to the viewing of, I believe, 62.5 million people on their small black and white boxes, there being at this time only a

handful of colour sets in the wealthier people's homes. In spite of this, I am told that the film has for quite a few years now been in the profit bracket. There would, of course, be nothing wrong at all with a nation-wide showing of any film under a pay-television scheme. Just think of the money we could have had in our pockets for only 50 cents in 62.5 million slot machines. I would have said then and I would say now that to show any film initially through the medium of television would be disastrous, though it may well be that now, fifteen years after the event, the position would be different.'

4. The first screen record of a Shakespearean stage production in the 1960s was an experimental 'electronivision' presentation in 1964 (the quater-centenary year) of John Gielgud's production of *Hamlet* on Broadway, starring Richard Burton. This was recorded by a number of small electronic cameras placed at strategic points in the theatre in order to transmit a normal, live performance, given before an audience. The camera-impulses were fed to a cine-recording unit, and the final film was made up from the recordings obtained during three separate performances. A thousand prints of the final film were made and shown in September 1964 for two days only in 976 cinemas coast to coast from New York to Los Angeles. The image had poor definition, and the sound was frequently indistinct. Richard Burton ordered the destruction of the prints after the two-day screening. The stage per-formance, which had opened in May with marked success, was given in rehearsal clothes, stripped of all extraneous trappings, like a final run-through for the actors. The setting was a bare platform with a brick backing. Richard Burton, wearing a black sweater and black trousers, dominated an unexciting cast, except for Eileen Herlie in her second screen appearance as the Queen. Burton interpreted Hamlet as highly-strung and angry, speaking the lines with a great intensity, but with a certain aloofness from the other characters.

5. This statement by Lord Birkett (Michael Birkett), together with my recorded conversation with Peter Hall which follows, were both published in the *Journal of the Society of Film and Television Arts*, Autumn 1969.

6. Interview by Sheridan Morley in *The Times*. The subsequent quotation comes from the same source.

II

Peter Brook's Film of *King Lear*

Speaking at the quatercentenary Shakespeare film congress organized by UNESCO in Paris, Peter Brook said, in effect, that Shakespeare was impossible to film; the compromises which had to be made were too fundamental. In a subsequent interview for *Sight and Sound* (Spring 1965) he said that he regarded the films made by Laurence Olivier and Orson Welles as actor-managers' pieces, with the camera the servant of the actors' performances in more or less traditional, nineteenth-century Shakespearean interpretations, greatly over-simplified; of these films he seems to prefer Welles's *Othello*, in parts, and Olivier's *Henry V*. Mankiewicz's *Julius Caesar* 'came from an intelligent reading of the play', and was a stepping-stone to the two best Shakespearean films, Kozintsev's academic but wholly consistent *Hamlet* ('the first time that there is the proper directorial approach of a man working from his own conviction of what the real threads of meaning are') and Kuro-sawa's 'great masterpiece', *The Castle of the Spider's Web*—a magnificent film, though 'it doesn't tackle the problem of how you make a film of Shakespeare which is a movie, and yet uses the fact that you've got a text which is continually changing gear'.

The problem of transferring Shakespeare from the delocalized environment of the stage boards to the specifically localized environment of the film set or location is that you lose the free association of image and thought which is the essence of Shakespeare's kaleidoscopic artistry and which had free play in the open theatre clear of all scenic obstruction.

The problem of filming Shakespeare is, how can you change gears, fluctuate between gears, styles and conventions as lightly and as deftly as the mental processes inside a person, which can be reflected by blank verse but not by the consistency of each single image?

With the coming of sound, especially, the cinema lost the capacity to suggest, and suggest alone: 'The mobility of *thought*, which the silent cinema had, is only just being recaptured in the cinema of Godard'. Godard's cinema, like Antonioni's, is an attempt to get out of the prison of photographic naturalism to a more Brechtian suggestion of multiplicity of meaning, arising from the very artificiality of the medium—actors performing on a stage before an audience, actors performing through a succession of photographic images projected onto a screen before an audience.

When you consider a major achievement of writing such as a play by Shakespeare, you are continually reinterpreting it. This object is there and it's like a sputnik, it turns round, and over the years different portions of it are nearer to you, different bits are further away. It's rushing past and you are peeling off these meanings. In that way a text is dynamic. The whole question of what Shakespeare intended doesn't arise, because what he has written not only carries more meanings than he consciously intended, but those meanings are altering in a mysterious way as the text moves through the centuries. If you dig into it you may find some new aspect, and yet you never seize the thing itself.

That was in 1965, and Brook's theoretical solution then was to use the multiple screen, which projected a number of separate images at once either as segments of the same collective image, or as a number of images projected simultaneously in counterpoint.

Four years later, in 1969, he was to make his first Shakespearean film production in association with Michael Birkett, the enterprising producer of such films as *The Caretaker*, Peter Hall's *A Midsummer Night's Dream*, and Peter Brook's own earlier film version of his theatre production of the *Marat-Sade*. In 1962 he had directed his outstanding stage production of the play at Stratford-upon-Avon, with Paul Scofield as Lear. Accounts of this theatre production— (for example, in the quotations published in the *Observer* of 16 December, 1962) by Brook's assistant, Charles Marowitz—revealed that Peter Brook had pondered over the production for a year, and saw it almost as the greatest of all dramas of the absurd—'Shakespeare's greatest play', 'a play about sight and blindness' culminating in the scene where the blinded Gloucester, intent on suicide, is led to believe he has fallen from a cliff height, and then encounters Lear, who, through suffering and madness, has gained true sight. The production involved a slow evolution towards the discovery of the play and its many key characters through rehearsal—stressing, apart from the central figures of Lear and Gloucester, the wide differences between the strength of Goneril, the weakness of Regan, Albany the expedient and Cornwall the sadistic, the villainy of Edmund and the innocence of Edgar, and the shining honesty of Kent. The lesser strands which unwind in the whole sub-plot about Gloucester eventually intertwine with the central strands in the main plot concerning Lear himself, and so make the complete play. Peter Brook was also conscious that the play had to have a very firm location and physical character; it is set in a pagan, pre-Christian society which had nevertheless reached a sufficient level of sophistication for what is said about social relationships to be viable alike for the Elizabethans and ourselves in the twentieth century. As Marowitz wrote:

> The world of this Lear, like Beckett's, is in a constant state of decomposition. The set-pieces consist of geometrical sheets of metal that are ginger with rust and corrosion. The costumes, dominantly leather, have been textured to suggest long and hard wear. The knights' tabards are peeling with long use; Lear's cape and coat are creased and blackened with time and weather. The furniture is rough wood, once sturdy but now decaying back into its hard, brown grain. Apart from the rust, the leather and the old wood, there is nothing but space—giant white flats opening on to a blank cyclorama.
>
> It is not so much Shakespeare in the style of Beckett as it is Beckett in the style of Shakespeare, for Brook believes that the cue for Beckett's bleakness was given by the merciless *King Lear*.[1]

When it was agreed to make the film, which is essentially a development of the original production for the theatre, prolonged discussions took place between Peter Brook and his producer, Lord Birkett, who was subsequently generous enough to record for me the following account of what took place during the planning stage.[2]

Each Shakespeare play is so different that it's almost impossible to talk about the problems of Shakespearean text-adaptation in a general sense at all. The two that I've made, *A Midsummer Night's Dream* and *King Lear*, were totally different in their approach; in the case of the *Dream* the text is extremely short by Shakespearean standards (only just over two hours, uncut and there wasn't any necessity to cut the text simply for length. More important, the play depends to a large extent upon its verbal patterns (it is, if you examine it, a very thin story in narrative terms). The placing of the scenes, the timing of the speeches, the tempo of the verse, are so miraculously calculated that one has to leave the text almost as it is. By this I don't mean that we didn't cut a single line; there are one or two passages where, in filming, we discovered that we were repeating ourselves in a way one wouldn't on the stage; so we cut a few lines, but very few indeed.

Lear, on the other hand, was at the opposite end of the scale; there the story itself forms a major part of the drama. At the same time, the uncut text of Lear runs for something like four and a quarter hours, so it was clear that we should have to do a fair amount of cutting, simply to achieve a workable length, but very little cutting in the sense of removing sub-plots, as is possible in other plays. In *Hamlet*, for example, Fortinbras often seems to disappear without too much damage to the structure of the play. But in Lear there is really no sub-plot that you *can* remove; everything is so integrated with the main themes of the play that it's impossible to make a clean extraction.

The nature of the text we used was the result of a very long, and I think very interesting, collaboration. We started simply by removing certain passages which we felt were completely unnecessary. But before setting down a workable text at all, we started to consider the actual nature of the words themselves —the idiom in which they're spoken. One of the films we admire most is Kurosawa's *Throne of Blood*, based on *Macbeth*. Kurosawa has used no Shakespearean text whatever, merely taken the story, the setting, and the themes of the play and written completely new words to go with them. This I suppose is easy enough in a foreign version of Shakespeare, since the text hasn't

136

the quality of Holy Writ that it has for the English-speaking world. There are usually several possible translations in foreign languages, and you can even make a new one. Nevertheless, we also recognised that a great deal of Shakespearean speech is extremely difficult going for a modern audience, particularly when the verse is at its most complex and full of conceits. So we made an experiment: we invited a very distinguished poet, Ted Hughes, to collaborate with us, gave him the text of *Lear* (slightly cut, from our first version) and suggested that he 'translate' it, treating it exactly as if it were a foreign classic; Goethe, Racine, or Dante, perhaps. We asked him to translate Shakespeare into his own idiom (not a self-consciously contemporary idiom, because there's really very little value in updating the language to make it sound like today—it's quite plain that the story does *not* take place in 1969)—to translate it into a language which seemed to him to be expressive of the story as he saw it, in his own right as a poet. The result of this was very intriguing and taught us a number of lessons about the text itself, about the nature of the play, about the themes concerned; but sooner or later it comes down to the fact that there are passages, obviously the greatest passages in the play, which have a force and emotional power that no translation, no paraphrase, can possibly match. Here it would obviously have been a shame to use anything except the most powerful language available, which was plainly Shakespeare's. Once using some of Shakespeare's text, it seemed unnatural not to use it throughout. Pastiche is not impossible (John Barton in his adaptation of the Henry VI plays at Stratford has shown that it's possible to write remarkably good Shakespearean pastiche with considerable weight and power behind it) but it seems unnecessary in Lear, where the language is of a much higher order than in *Henry VI*. Certain simplifications are possible: one can always change a word if it's too obscure, as long as one can find a word which conveys the same meaning, and has the same sort of ring as the original. But by and large, in spite of this very interesting experiment—some remarkable work by Ted Hughes—we decided to stick to the original language. Thereafter, before preparing the text, Peter Brook wrote a treatment of the play in narrative form, with no dialogue whatever, simply to seek out its essential nature, the themes behind it. From this document we worked out a very precise story-line and a very careful estimate of the weight we wanted to put on each episode, each character, and each theme in the piece. After this, it was very much easier to choose and cut the text, not to fit in with a new or eccentric interpretation of the play, but with what we conceived to be its essentials. Only as a result of this work did we finally carve out the final script, and even that was altered considerably in the course of production; certain events took on an extra importance as we came to shoot them, and certain events seemed to be less impressive by comparison, so that a certain amount of adaptation went on throughout. We even transposed lines from one character to another, so I suspect that no Shakespearean purist is likely to approve of us!

When we came to consider how the words should actually be treated on the screen, we realised that the power of Shakespeare's writing—particularly its evocative power—is so enormous that although one can find images which may seem appropriate, images that are in no way at odds with the text, sometimes images become unnecessary or even unwanted— they can actually get between the audience and the power of the words. It would be easy at such moments merely to cut to a blank screen (an empty sky, an open field, or simply spacing) but this isn't quite good enough; a totally blank screen is, of course, impossible, it simply looks as if the machinery has broken down. (Spacing on a sound-track—genuine silence—is not silence but death; it's a dead thing. To make silence work on the screen you have to invent a noise which gives the impression of silence.) In the same way, to create a blank visually on the screen you have to invent an image which gives the *impression* of blankness, and therefore it can't quite be blank—something has to be there. Also, it is often self-conscious deliberately to pan off, or cut away from, a character who is speaking, simply in order to leave the words more room. There has to be a way of doing it which appears natural and at the same time achieves the desired effect of leaving the audience free to get the full weight of the words. It's interesting that we found shooting profiles and the backs of people's heads at such moments very much more 'liberating' than a full-face close-up. We used a lot of full-face close-ups in *A Midsummer Night's Dream* and there's no doubt—I dare say Peter Hall would agree with this to a certain extent—that there are moments when the sheer sight of the face and its lips moving comes between you and the words the face is saying. Even with the most restrained style of acting, in which nobody could be accused of mouthing, the big close-up can at times form a sort of barrier between the little private screen in one's head, in which Shakespeare's evocative words are making pictures, and the real screen in the cinema. Of course, this applies really only to those passages where the emotional pressure is at its most intense. And yet, in a paradoxical way, it's at those moments we found in Lear that one could afford to be very much closer in on people, very much closer to the faces, than in the more ordinary passages.

Another problem that every Shakespearean film-maker faces is the décor (by which I mean sets, costumes, make-ups, props, locations), how to make a physical world for the film which is at one with the text and, at the same time, avoids the sort of operatic hangover that bedevils so much Shakespeare. So often classics seem to be very demonstrative in their sets and clothes. There seems to be a feeling that one owes it to the dramatist, to the Bard himself, to provide the richest and lushest sets and costumes. Yet it's very rare to find a Shakespearean play or film in which the world that the characters inhabit is genuinely believable and genuinely consistent. We wanted in Lear to achieve the same sort of effortless effect as a modern thriller. Nobody in a modern thriller remarks on the clothes worn by the policemen, the car driven by the murderer or the set in which the suspect lives, because if these things are properly done they are so natural that people accept them quite subconsciously. In the case of a period film, the further back in time you go, the more difficult it is to achieve this sort of naturalism, or realism, whatever the word should be. Not only is the idiom of the words very much removed from our own time, but in the case of *King Lear*, although it hasn't an exact date in history, the story must have occurred some time between the Romans leaving Britain and William the Conqueror arriving. Somewhere, in other words, in the Dark Ages. The two dangers that Brook and I wanted to avoid were 'authenticity' and 'timelessness'. Both of these phrases are much used in publicity handouts, and both seem to me to be less than helpful. 'Authenticity' seems to invoke an enormous amount of detailed and painstaking research, devoted to making the film as exact as possible in regard to the surviving records of a period. Now this may be some delight to the historian but has nothing whatever to do with the convincing of an audience. One wants an audience to accept the world in which a story is happening as being plausible, real, something with which they can feel familiar from the moment the film starts. The one place where this is unlikely is a museum. 'Authenticity' amounts to making a film as a museum piece. The other danger, 'timelessness', is merely the danger of a cop-out; if you don't know enough about a period, or if you don't have clear enough ideas about the atmosphere you want to build up, then you find something so neutral that it amounts to no period and no atmosphere. In between this limbo and the museum lies the only possible answer for filming a Shakespeare play (any Shakespeare play; here I think one can generalise), that is, to invent a setting which has a period and a style and a flavour of its own, a setting dictated not by the nature of a particular moment in history, but by the nature of the play that you're dealing with. Brook and I approached the problem simply by considering the nature of the buildings, the clothes, the props, the landscapes, very carefully in relation to the play itself and the sort of civilisation that it implied. We share a magpie instinct for picking up styles and flavours from all periods of history, and after months of discussion we begin to define the world in which we wanted to set *King Lear*. We could neither of us have expressed it exactly, but when we set out to look for locations, when we looked at the first drawings for the castles, at the first props, at the first horses, even, we knew very certainly whether things were right or wrong, and we rarely disagreed. It was uncanny how often our choice fell on the same spoon, the same stirrup, the same piece of landscape, without ever attempting to codify our conclusions.

Out of this concern to make, or at least invent, a real and plausible world, comes the next problem—the choice of cast and the way in which they should play their parts and indeed speak the lines. In the case of Lear, we had the advantage that Brook had already done a very notable stage production for the Royal Shakespeare Company, with Paul Scofield, Irene Worth and many distinguished people in it; at the same time, we had no intention of filming a stage production. Nevertheless, several of the actors concerned had been so good and, we thought, would look so right on the screen that they were chosen again. Obviously Paul Scofield himself was one of our reasons for undertaking *King Lear* in the first place. Irene Worth as Goneril, Alan Webb as Gloucester, Tom Fleming as Kent, were also chosen from the original stage production, simply because they had already made these characters so powerfully real that it would have been senseless to look further. For the rest of the cast, we suddenly found ourselves rather in sympathy with the Hollywood moguls who are so often maligned for 'type-casting'. On the stage, and particularly with a company crammed with talent like the Royal Shakespeare Company or the National Theatre, it's possible simply to equate the talents and the variety of an actor with a part that needs casting; it's possible to get away with a fine performance which at close range would not necessarily look convincing. When it comes to the screen, however, it may be that the very first shot of a character carries no dialogue with it but is close and revealing. The very look of the face has to be convincing; the actors must *be* the character, with no other aid than the clothes he wears and the make-up of his face. Of course, the main complaint about type-casting is that it's the type which matters and not the talent, so that actors are never allowed to extend their range. But if one restricts one's search to people of talent and sensitivity, then 'type-casting' is not such a discreditable business, but is almost an essential for conviction on the screen.

Then comes the problem of how the actors are actually to speak lines which in many cases were clearly designed for a 'projected', almost rhetorical, form of delivery. This is a problem that's not special to the film, it's special, I suppose, to the year in which one's working, because everybody recognises the necessity of making what is a very old-fashioned idiom alive and meaningful for a modern audience. The device sometimes resorted to on the stage, modernising the delivery, of trying to find in Shakespearean verse the nearest modern idiomatic equivalent, is usually disastrous. It doesn't bring Shakespeare up to date at all, it merely gives the impression of somebody in 1969 desperately struggling with words that are not his and with which he has some trouble in expressing himself. It merely underlines how far away from today the *idiom* of Shakespeare is, but conceals how close to today is the essence of the plays. The verse must be spoken for what it is, using the rhythms and the flavours that it has, and presumably always had, trying to find an emotional truth within this idiom and this structure. Unless an actor can find this truth, the verse is liable to come out either phoney or merely dull. And if this search for the truth of a character, for the truth of expression within the verse, is important on the stage, how much more important it is in a film, where the close-up must be the most revealing form of expression that acting has ever had to encompass.

This search for an expressive truth is also the clue to another problem in Shakespeare—those speeches which were meant to be spoken not merely very loudly, but projected with a deal of dramatic panache. Pistol in *Henry IV* speaks in a parody of the heroic style of the age, but even allowing that Shakespeare found that style often too high-flown and melodramatic (Hamlet's advice to the Player King provides further evidence of this), there are nevertheless passages where a high rhetorical effect is obviously intended. When one comes to film these passages, if they are delivered in the full rhetorical style and at full volume one has two really unfortunate alternatives: either to allow the screen to bend under the weight of what seems a quite unnatural and operatic delivery, or to withdraw the camera rapidly into extreme longshot, where one isn't embarrassed by what otherwise might appear as overacting. I don't mean that a longshot is always ineffective in the circumstances —everybody remembers Olivier in *Henry V* using it to great effect, particularly in the patriotic battle speeches—but it can be selfconscious if it's used merely in self-defence, so to speak. Here again, I find that the answer lies more in re-examining the text itself, to discover whether in fact the exclamatory rhetoric is an essential element or whether there is not a way of reconceiving it in terms of pure character rather than of pure effect. It was surprising in *Lear* how much this sort of agonising reappraisal led to new and worthwhile discoveries about the text itself, and in particular about the whole nature of the storm scene.

All these problems, of course, crop up once again at the editing stage. Here one finds that Shakespearean verse, and Shakespearean prose too, for the matter of that, has certain very defined and strong rhythms which sometimes run counter to normal editing technique. Since, mercifully, it's impossible to give any rules of conduct for normal editing, it's equally impossible to pontificate about Shakespearean exceptions. Of course, every editor balances the tempo of his cutting not only to the visuals, but to the sound track as he knows it'll be at the time of dubbing, with all the effects and extra tracks added. Nevertheless, in Shakespeare there are sometimes certain echoes, certain pauses, which the text absolutely demands; if these are not fulfilled, it leaves an unsatisfactory impression. Peter Hall and I found on *A Midsummer Night's Dream* that there were several passages where, looking at the picture on a movieola, without any sound, the cutting pattern seemed to be perfect. Hearing the sound track on its own, the rhythms of the speech also seemed to be fine. When the two were run together, however, the result seemed unsatisfactory. We had to evolve a style of cutting which was equally fair to the rhythm of the verse and to the rhythm of the pictures. In the long run there always seems to be a solution, but our experience was that it took twice as long as usual to find it.

I said earlier on that I didn't think it was possible to talk in general terms about the filming of Shakespeare, so different was each play from the next, and yet I seem to have been generalising a lot. Perhaps this is because I've only tried two, and they have been so enormously different that when something special has occurred in both it's almost irresistible to generalise about it; but I think that all such generalisations, and especially mine, should be taken with a large pinch of salt. Perhaps, after all, making films based on Shakespeare is not so very different from making films of any other sort, except in one important respect: the author is of such stature that he is likely to remain in the ascendant over everybody else concerned with the picture. It isn't so much a matter of respect for his name and fame (he can be treated worse than a living author in some ways!) as the inescapable fact that most of the time one cannot add to his work, one can merely hope to interpret it as powerfully as possible.

The film was shot during the winter of 1968-9, mainly on location in North Jutland, Denmark. Here a large walled compound was built to represent Goneril's castle, where a great part of the action takes place before Lear loses his reason and goes out raging into the storm. The climactic scene, in which Lear's madness turns to an inspired sanity when he meets the dispossessed and blinded Gloucester, is played on a flat stretch of sand by the sea. It is here that he is found by Cordelia's men, reunited with her, and finally captured along with her by the forces of Goneril and Regan. Cordelia is hanged, and Lear dies after carrying Cordelia's body out upon the open, deserted shore.

Paul Scofield's Lear has evolved over the years to become one of the great performances of the century in this most demanding of all parts—Peter Brook has described the character as a mountain whose summit has never been reached. By the time the film was made it was therefore a fully matured interpretation, every nuance of which was known to the actor. Lear, Scofield said once, 'made me push my voice into places it had never been before'. It became essentially the voice of an old man; it has the gruffness, chestiness, the occasional break of pitch which reveals great age, though it carries still the strength of a man used to exercising absolute power and brooking no interference with his will. In his rage, Lear can still muster the strength to overturn one of the great tables in Goneril's castle, or carry the strangled body of Cordelia out upon the shore. Scofield's Lear represents power on the edge of disintegration and decrepitude, to which Lear finally succumbs through madness, a form of purgation which brings him, during the last hours of his life, a wisdom and humanity he has never before experienced.

In the shooting script, the opening of the film is described as follows: [3]

Suddenly, without any fuss, the KING, old, energetic, impatient, is there, climbing on to his throne.

LEAR: Give me the map.

GLOUCESTER brings it him. For a moment, we see side by side the two aged heads: both in their eighties, GLOUCESTER fussy, anxious and LEAR powerful, set. LEAR unrolls the map as he looks round the room, examining everyone present, missing nothing, enjoying protracting the tension. What we see is his world. Every element present is charged with potentially explosive power, yet everything is held in its place. All is in order, LEAR's order. His authority is complete. Every element in the room, every element in himself is subjected to his control. Age has in no way diminished him, nor the structure he has created. He has let go of nothing, In fact, so fixed is his scheme of things, that it requires no outward display of threat or splendour to assert itself.

He states the intention of the ceremony. He is dividing the kingdom into three, giving it over to younger people, shedding his own load. Coolly appraising his married children, he gives his precise reason—it is to avoid conflict in the future. He further explains that the marriage of his third daughter either to the Duke of Burgundy or to the King of France, both of whom are now present, is an intrinsic part of his grand design. Again, he allows expectancy to rise. Now, he calls on the daughters to make a declaration of love to him. This is no surprise. GONERIL prepared for such a ceremony steps forward and with great eloquence makes formal expression of her devotion to her father. 'Dearer than eyesight, space and liberty', she says, unconsciously putting into words the very qualities that this court lacks. But its old machinery is turning over smoothly: her phrases are heard with appreciation; LEAR reads out the description of the fine lands she and her family are being bequeathed.

Next, it is REGAN'S turn and she acquits herself equally well. There are profound differences between the two sisters, but they do not yet emerge. At first view, we notice the points in common: they share the same poise, the same social gifts. 'We are made of the same metal', says REGAN. Her gracious speech brings the prepared bequest, but as she returns to her seat and her husband squeezes her hand, all excesses of satisfaction are concealed. LEAR turns to his third daughter. Now a new quality comes into his voice, a deeply guarded tenderness. CORDELIA steps forward, as formal and

A MIDSUMMER NIGHT'S DREAM Great Britain (1969). Director, Peter Hall

The Lovers: Lysander (David Warner), Hermia (Helen Mirren), Helena (Diana Rigg), Demetrius (Michael Jayston)

The Lovers

The Clowns: Bottom (Paul Rogers), Quince (Sebastian Shaw), Snout (Bill Travers), Flute (John Normington), Snug (Clive Swift), Starveling (Donald Eccles)

Fairies and Elves
Titania (Judi
Dench)

Oberon (Ian
Richardson) puts
the magic juice
into the eyes of
Titania, while she
sleeps with Botto

Puck (Ian Holm)
in Theseus'
Palace

KUMONOSU-DJO
(*The Castle of the Spider's Web*);
THE THRONE OF
BLOOD. (Japan
1957). Director,
Akira Kurosawa

Washizu (Macbeth:
Toshiro Mifune)
and Yoshiaki
Miki (Banquo:
Minoru Chiaki)
in the forest of the
Spider's Web

Washizu and Miki
meet the Weird
Woman of the
Forest (Chieko
Naniwa)

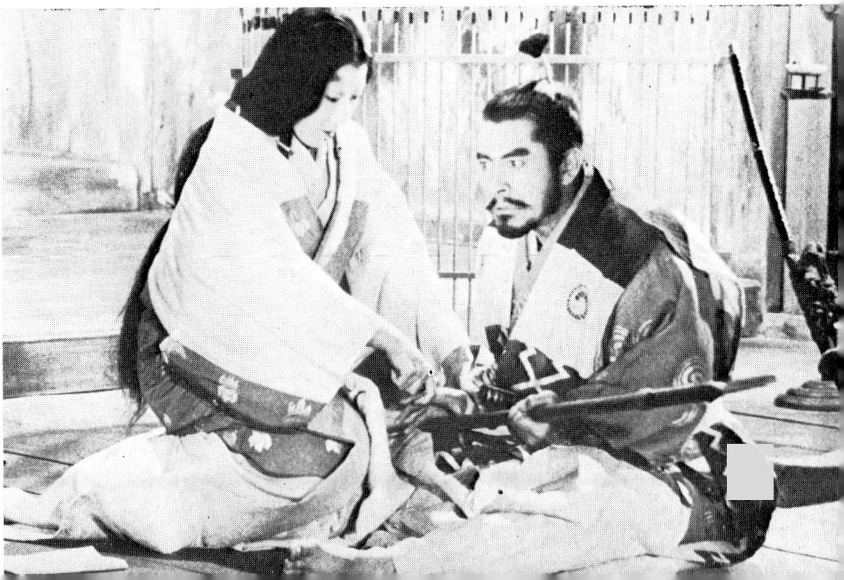

Washizu and Asaji
(Lady Macbeth:
Isuzu Yamada),
at the time of the
murder of Duncan

Washizu seeks the prophecies of the Weird Woman for the second time

Asaji washing her hands

Noh masks corresponding to expressions for Washizu and Asaji

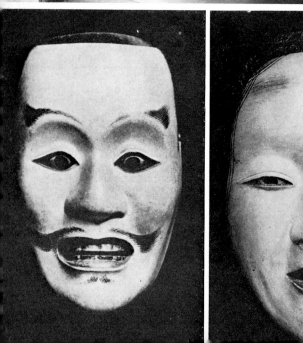

Washizu

The death of Washizu

KING LEAR (Great Britain 1970).
Director, Peter Brook

Lear (Paul Scofield)

Goneril (Irene Worth)
and Regan (Susan Engel)

The Castle

Lear

Goneril

The landscape
of the film

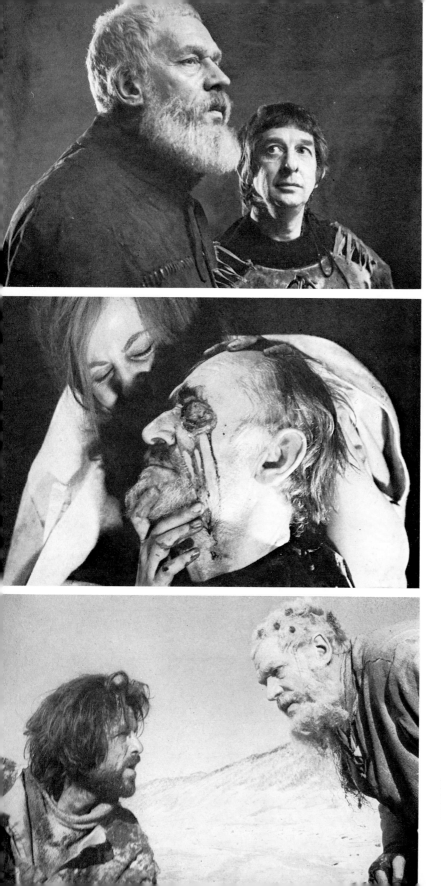

Lear and the
Fool (Jack
MacGowran)

Gloucester (Alan
Webb) and
Regan

Lear and
Kent (Tom
Fleming)

impersonal as the others had been. FRANCE and BURGUNDY lean forward expectantly. There is a long silence.

LEAR: Speak.

CORDELIA: Nothing, my lord.

LEAR: Nothing?

CORDELIA: Nothing.

CORDELIA and LEAR confront one another: two refusals, two extremes. CORDELIA refusing a game and a system which her honesty rejects: LEAR refusing her challenge, blind to its meaning, recognising only that his absolute rightness is menaced. Her obstinacy matches his strength, because it is of the same material. We read this in their faces, CORDELIA has a Lear-like will, LEAR has a Cordelia-like refusal of compromise. It is a head-on clash. Both natures must go all their way. A collision cannot be avoided. Court officials are at a loss, Knights amazed, the ceremony broken, order overthrown. With LEAR's violent explosive reaction, the CAMERA for the first time moves abruptly. In a torrent of rush decisions, LEAR improvises a new plan. The balanced and orderly division into three is scrapped, instead, impulsively he carves the kingdom into two. For himself he will only keep a hundred knights and will live alternately with his two sons-in-law. The Earl of Kent, through the disorder, makes an attempt to reason: he speaks diplomatically, but is at once cut off by LEAR, who silences him with dangerous menace. KENT too is a man of extremes: 'Lear is mad!' he explodes and adds the sensational, unforgiveable gibe, 'Old man!' LEAR has no choice: his power and potency must now be publicly reaffirmed. He banished KENT on pain of death. A heavy silence weighs over the room, no one moves or speaks. LEAR regains his self-control and turns sharply on the DUKE OF BURGUNDY. He points to the still-motionless CORDELIA. 'What is the least you require in dower with her?' he asks. BURGUNDY cautiously answers that he expects neither more nor less than had been offered before. 'Her price has fallen', says the King bluntly. CORDELIA does not react. BURGUNDY attempts to bargain, but the KING interrupts him. 'Take her or leave her'. BURGUNDY is shifty. 'You have lost a husband', he says, confused. At once FRANCE steps forward, splendidly contemptuous, and takes her hand. LEAR gives her to him with equal decision and he leaves the throne room, still the master, still in control. It is as though nothing has changed.

The development of the action brings the characters together in the barren, misty countryside, with its covering of mud and snow. Goneril and Regan hatch their first plot to control Lear in a large, heavy-wheeled coach as they jolt along the unmade roads; Gloucester

145

and Kent, with armed escort, drive off in another coach—'We have seen the best of our time,' says Gloucester. When they arrive at Gloucester's castle, Edmund is there obsequiously to welcome his natural father. Kent leaves the castle still under escort, having taken his leave of Gloucester and his two sons. Edgar, the innocent-minded legitimate son, admires the worldliness of his elder brother, the illegitimate Edmund, laughing at his claim, as a bastard, to be 'rough and lecherous'.

Kent, meanwhile, sets on the two men accompanying him and kills them. With the fanaticism of absolute honesty, he disguises himself as a peasant in order to return to tend the King who has banished him. He is there ready to meet him, in fact, as Lear returns with a hunting party made up of his rowdy knights, whose presence in Goneril's castle is made evident by the damage they have done to her carpets and furniture. Lear, calling out for his dinner as he dismounts in the courtyard, takes Kent into his service. In the scene that follows in the dining hall, Oswald, Goneril's principal servant, is insolent to Lear and is struck by Kent for his pains, while the Fool entertains Lear and the knights with his veiled home truths which they cannot understand. The all-licensed Fool becomes the only messenger of truth to whom Lear will give any attention. The Fool has a secret power over him.

In their own chamber, Goneril overrules her weak husband, Albany, whose only wish is to avoid trouble. Unable to endure the drunken excesses of her father's retinue, Goneril enrages him by demanding that he dismiss a quantity of his knights. Lear oversets the table, spilling the mess of the meal's remains on the floor. 'Darkness and devils; saddle my horses,' he cries, while the knights, like a group of drunken hooligans, smash up everything in sight. Lear calls down sterility upon Goneril, but she opposes him with a will equal to his own—father and daughter each blindly convinced of their own righteousness. Lear clambers into his coach, weeping with anger; the Fool sits exhausted beside him. The script reveals the importance of their relationship:

> LEAR is deeply thoughtful, open perhaps for the very first time to glimpses of self-reproach. 'I did her wrong', he murmurs. The FOOL jolts on the cushions beside him, trying weakly to cheer the King with poor jokes. One sees the deep

intimacy that underlies their relationship. LEAR does not speak directly to the FOOL, but in his presence, he is capable of speaking out his deepest thoughts and dreads. 'Oh let me not be mad', he prays. 'Not mad, sweet heavens.'

In the darkness, they jog on, neither speaking further.

Oswald precedes him to Regan's castle with Goneril's letter of warning. It is dusk when Lear's cavalcade arrives; the castle is blacked out; Regan and her husband Cornwall are visiting Gloucester.

Meanwhile, another scene of dispossession is taking place in Gloucester's castle; Edmund divides Gloucester and Edgar by a trick, and Edgar flees the castle: he narrowly escapes capture, and disguises himself as a half-naked madman. Gloucester, as deceived now about Edgar's love as Lear was about Cordelia's, believes Edmund to be his loyal son, and says as much to his guests, Regan and Cornwall. This sets Edmund in a new light to Cornwall and Regan. Kent, attempting with violence to forestall Oswald's delivery of Goneril's letter to Regan, is put in the stocks for his pains.

Lear, deserted now by some of his knights, finally arrives at Gloucester's castle. He has travelled all night, and is shocked to find the man he regards as his servant confined in the stocks, his beard covered in icicles. As the script put it:

> It is another blow to LEAR's respect, another 'violent outrage'. Again, his reason shudders, something dark and wild is pressing up to the surface. He controls himself, tells the others to stay and goes himself to beat on the main door of the house.

Gloucester becomes the unhappy intermediary between the 'hot duke' and Lear, who is striving to retain his self-control. Regan finally receives her father on the threshold of the castle, not inviting him in, treating him like a child. As she tries to put him off, saying she is not in readiness to entertain him properly, Goneril arrives, and the sisters immediately draw together to oppose him. Their resolution to reduce him to utter, isolated dependency finally drives him out of his mind. In spite of the storm, he mounts the coachman's seat and lashes the horses into a frenzied gallop. Only the Fool is inside. The coach crashes on through the mounting storm until the wheels break against the stones and the carriage overturns. Lear, clutching the Fool to

him, mounts a horse and penetrates deeper and deeper into the wild
no-man's-land, drenched with rain and with lightning. The knights
are dispersed and gone; only Kent searches for him on horseback.
The script goes on:

89 EXT. HEATH. NIGHT. The storm grows more and more savage.
Gradually, it will be impossible to tell how much it is the real world
undergoing this epic convulsion, how much the landscape is the inside
of LEAR's mind. For the images become less and less narrative,
more and more strange, surrealist though never apparently fantastic.
The ground cracks open, roots painfully are wrenched to the surface,
roofs are carried away, walls burst outwards, great doors fly open,
shutters snap their catches and bang apart, flames mount amongst
branches, wells overflow their pitch-black content, but out of the
gashes and scars in the earth come scorpions, ants, spiders, snakes.
    All the time LEAR moves forward, crossing the black landscape.
In the sequence of SHOTS, two views intermingle, the ferocious
images that LEAR sees, the equally frightening but more prosaic
viewpoint of the FOOL, for whom the storm is nothing but wind
and water and cold. LEAR now is in touch with the elements, he
speaks to the sky, whilst the FOOL clings to his legs. LEAR is with
the wind, with the thunderbolts, they are his terrors, they are his
vengeance—the heavens, he cries, are a great bowl of creation where
float the spermatozoa that make for ungrateful men. Spill your
contents then, he cries. He has reached a unique condition of total
energy, freed by a total rejection of all things human: only vast
impersonal forces are his brothers, only they can be free of the mean-
ness of mankind. Yet locked to his feet is a voice that he ignores, a
voice of a frightened creature that only wants a roof—ask pity of your
daughters, it now says, anything to be dry.
    Suddenly, a figure wades and struggles out of the darkness—
KENT. He has lost his horse and now all he can do is to try to en-
velop LEAR in his cloak. . . .
    The images are hallucinatory. As LEAR is being led by KENT
towards the shelter of a miserable abandoned hovel what he sees lit
in flashes of lightning could well be a rock, a stone, a stump, a bush—
but could equally well be some agonising human shape, a limb, a
face, a burnt child, a screaming mouth. And the alternately black and
fiery horizon could be that of a scene of war. At the door of the hovel,
LEAR refuses to enter. Go in, he urges, the others go in. I wish to
be alone to pray. KENT tells the FOOL to enter. LEAR oblivious
of the rain streaming down over him, has a moment of quiet, an
instant of reflection. Peering into the strange middle distance,
peopled with shadows, he utters a prayer for all the homeless.
Suddenly they have become real to him. He has reached a moment of
great realisation and he says to himself with wonder, 'I have taken
too little care of this'.

148

Kent is the only rational man left in the group, but Lear is moving towards true perception through the experience of hallucination, while both the Fool and Edgar (playing the lunatic with ever-increasing dedication) hover on the undefined borderline between sanity and insanity. Edgar is represented as 'possessed', acting like a medium in his utterance of veiled and gnomic truths.

The outer plot takes shape: Regan begins to want Edmund sexually; Gloucester is condemned because he has deserted Cornwall's side to search out and succour the King. In a potting-shed under the castle walls, to which Gloucester and Kent have taken Lear and the companions from whom he will not be parted for momentary shelter, the hallucinatory trial of Goneril and Regan is conducted. Kent lifts Lear, now collapsed into sleep, into a wagon to take him towards Dover. Cordelia, in France, has already been sent word of the trouble between him and his daughters. Gloucester, returning to his castle, is placed under arrest by Cornwall, who has taken over command. The bloody scene of Gloucester's blinding follows, with its emphasis on the innate sadism of both Regan and her husband. The servants are appalled; one even stages resistance and wounds Cornwall, but he is killed by Regan. Gloucester, demented with agony, is driven out, like Lear, to 'smell his way to Dover', where the French forces are known to have landed. Gloucester's servants, terrified by what has happened, have applied broken eggs to the sockets of his eyes to ease the bleeding. It is Edgar, still initially crazed, who comes to his help as he crawls through the mud; the madman and the blind man go off together in the dawn. Their goal is Dover.

Edmund and Goneril are in bed together; later, when Albany discovers her, she mocks him for his impotence: 'the difference between man and man', she murmurs. Edmund has been created by Cornwall the new Duke of Gloucester; he is excited by the prospect of union with Regan when Cornwall dies of his wound. Edmund is now master of the English forces.

Lear's litter reaches Dover; he slips out unnoticed while Kent surveys the French ships offshore. Then follow the crucial scenes of revelation when, after Gloucester's hallucinatory suicide by falling from the 'cliffs' of Dover, he is discovered by the mad King on the shore.

GLOUCESTER is listening to the waves. LEAR very close by murmurs, 'Ha, Goneril with a white beard'. GLOUCESTER turns his head. 'I know that voice.' He listens and LEAR goes on speaking, not in anger, but in profound bitterness. 'Is't not the King?' GLOUCESTER asks wonderingly. 'Every inch a King', the voice returns.

LEAR sits on the sand beside GLOUCESTER. The two ashen old men are alone by the water's edge on the vast deserted beach. GLOUCESTER reaches for the King's hand to kiss. LEAR wipes it. 'It smells,' he says, 'of mortality.' GLOU-CESTER turns his empty sockets to LEAR. 'Do you know me?' he asks. 'I remember thine eyes well enough,' the King answers. LEAR shakes his head and tells GLOUCESTER no eyes are needed to tell how the world goes. Ears are enough, when everything is upside down. For to the King all has become clear. Order—the very order of which he was the structure and the guarantee—is no order at all—the division between judge and thief, judge and whore, miser and cheat are all meaningless. No. There are no criminals. Be like a politician, he states. Get glass eyes and see things as they aren't. And anyway, he adds, I know you well enough, you are GLOUCESTER. The whole encounter with the King has been unendurable for GLOUCESTER, and at this he breaks down completely. As one old man comforts the other, from a distance French soldiers and the English attendants quietly approach.

When the French soldiers searching for the King finally find him, he eludes them, and wades out into the sea before they can catch up with him. He awakes in Cordelia's tent, his spirit calm, his self-knowledge absolute. 'I am old, and foolish.'

But Edmund, at the peak of his power, is already overreaching himself, not least in having excited sexual rivalry in Goneril and Regan. Albany is interested only in repelling an invasion by France. Edmund sleeps with Regan. Edgar's relationship to his father, whom he tries to draw away from the battle between the French and the English, is much like that of Cordelia and Lear. It is in the spirit of quietude that he finally dies, worn out with strife, as the battle rages around him.

Quietude, too, has reached Lear and Cordelia, when they become Edmund's prisoners.

LEAR and CORDELIA are protected by a private circle of calm. Nothing can penetrate nor disturb it. Its existence is EDMUND's greatest threat: it is something he cannot under-stand. His face is twisted in a way we have not seen before:

he is beginning to be locked in the pattern he has lived by: his features are setting themselves into a map of anger and hate.

LEAR: No, no, no, no; come, let's away to prison:
　　We two alone will sing like birds i' th' cage.
　　When thou dost ask me blessing, I'll kneel down,
　　And ask of thee forgiveness. So we'll live,
　　And pray, and sing, and tell old tales, and laugh
　　At gilded butterflies; and hear poor rogues
　　Talk of court news, and we'll talk with them too,
　　Who loses, and who wins, who's in, who's out;
　　And take upon's the mystery of things,
　　As if we were God's spies. And we'll wear out
　　In a walled prison, packs and sects of great ones,
　　That ebb and flow by th' moon.

The wheel comes full circle. Goneril and Regan kill each other, and Edmund is slain in combat by Edgar, but not before he has ordered Cordelia to be hanged.

EXT. PEBBLE DESERT. A great overhead shot. From the sea, the desert of pebbles stretches inland as far as the skyline.
　　From the cliffs a few figures straggle down. From another point, LEAR, carrying CORDELIA in his arms, is walking away, towards the plain. Even from far off we can hear he is uttering a terrible animal cry.
　　On and on he goes, until he comes to a stop and sinks to the ground.

EXT. PEBBLE DESERT. DAY. LEAR is bending over CORDELIA. This last hammer blow from nowhere leaves him with no philosophy, no understanding, just an ultimate cry of pain and bewilderment. It cannot have happened, it cannot be true.
　　In the distance, a tiny knot forms, KENT, ALBANY, EDGAR.
　　KENT approaches, kneels by LEAR. For a moment, LEAR sees him clearly and knows him, not only as his SERVANT, but also seeing through his disguise, recognises him as KENT. Then, after this instant of lucidity, his mind wanders. CORDELIA and a memory of the FOOL merge into one object for him, a life that will never come back.

LEAR: Never, never, never, never, never.

Then even in this darkness, he sees something move. 'Look,' he cries, 'her lips! Look, look!' He points and dies.
　　Does he see CORDELIA's spirit or is this a final madness? We can never know.
　　EDGAR runs to him, suddenly young and clumsy, trying to help. KENT turns on him with a titanic, cosmic rage. 'He hates him

that would on the rack of this tough world stretch him out longer.'

ALBANY is ineffective in these circumstances. Although he is now heir to the throne, true to his nature, he withdraws, saying to EDGAR and KENT, 'You both rule.'

But KENT's way is clear. Motionless, shattered, like a powerful tree struck by lighting—or a strong man after a stroke—he speaks his intention: he will be following his master.

EDGAR sees that the future is his. He tries to understand what was and what will be. He speaks to the CAMERA—words full of enigma —enigmas he has lived but has still to understand.

EDGAR: The weight of these sad times we must obey,
Speak what we feel, not what we ought to say,
The oldest have borne most: we that are young,
Shall never see so much, nor live so long.

He is alone in the desert. Then this picture also vanishes, until nothing has left a trace.

Notes to Chapter 11

1. Peter Brook told me in Paris in 1964 that he possessed a recorded television production of the play with Paul Scofield. This recording was never shown in England.

2. 'King Lear: from Page to Screen: Michael Birkett talks to Roger Manvell.' Originally published in the *Journal of the Society of Film and Television Arts* (Autumn 1969).

3. Reproduced by kind permission of Lord Birkett and Peter Brook.

12

Perspectives

There have been so far many kinds of Shakespearean adaptation for the sound screen. They represent different approaches, ranging from the camera-record of a production already well-matured on the stage (such as *Othello*, with Laurence Olivier), to the full screen adaptation of a considered version of the text, such as Laurence Olivier's *Hamlet*, Joseph Mankiewicz's *Julius Caesar*, Peter Brook's *King Lear*, Orson Welles's special projection of the character of Falstaff in *Chimes at Midnight*, or Kozintsev's Pasternak-Shakespearean *Hamlet*. And further out from all those stands Kurosawa's *The Castle of the Spider's Web* which, while entirely discarding the dramatic verse of *Macbeth* and totally changing its venue, nevertheless most successfully distils the atmosphere and imagery of Shakespeare's play in the form of a highly stylized re-creation of its essential action in a traditional Japanese setting. Yet it is this film, so completely removed from Shakespeare's actual text, which has won the warmest tributes from such dedicated Shakespeareans as Grigori Kozintsev, Peter Hall and Peter Brook.

On the more obvious level of screen presentation, the dynamically fluid medium of the film can in most respects reflect admirably the general rhythm and tempo of Shakespeare's dramatic action and atmosphere. He is a dynamic, not a static playwright—in the sense that Corneille, for example, is static. The ability of camera and microphone to alternate panoramic, or larger-scale action, with closeness and intimacy of observation suits the rapid changes of dramatic scale which Shakespeare himself explored on the free and open stages of the Elizabethan theatre. But contemporary screen techniques have also shown (notably in the films, for example, of Bergman and Antonioni) that visual dynamics are not the only valid form of cinema—indeed, the more penetrating observation of character may well justify prolonged periods of concentrated watchfulness, with little camera-movement or insistent cutting. Shakespeare's profounder verse needs such moments of visual 'rest', so that the speech, closely 'observed' and listened to, may work unhindered into the consciousness of the audience—though without, one would hope, complete loss of visual interest. The significance of the speech can indeed be 'up-pointed' by the very closeness of this visual observation, and the consequent intimacy of expression which this makes possible for the actor. The close shot makes any touch of the false histrionics for which the stage was formerly responsible as ugly as it is superfluous. This can be true alike for Shakespeare's own words and for such careful, sensitive translations as Pasternak has made.

But this is a period in which the discovery of new 'meaning' in established works, as well as experiments in presentation on both stage and screen, must affect the handling of Shakespeare. We may agree or disagree with Welles's interpretation of *Macbeth* or Peter Hall's conception of *A Midsummer Night's Dream*. Peter Brook's reconception of the *Dream* on the stage at Stratford-upon-Avon in 1970 might well form the basis for a striking film. Though films of this more experimental kind, or those conceived after the manner of Kurosawa's 'distillation' of *Macbeth*, will probably remain rare, nevertheless the outer 'fringe' of Shakespearean film-making, it is to be hoped, will have some future on the screen. By these means new significance can be found in the familiar words, and another dimension of thought and feeling be added to our cumulative interpretation of the plays. If the film, as a virtually new medium for their presentation, can in any way help expand the recognition of what still lies to be discovered in Shakespeare's writing, it will have made its contribution—as well as bringing the plays to the attention of millions of people through the cinema and television whom production in the living theatre can seldom or never reach.

Filmography

This list with credits of the principal films adapted from Shakespeare since 1929 is given in the order in which the films are discussed in the book.

THE TAMING OF THE SHREW. U.S.A. 1929. Production, the Pickford Corporation; the Elton Corporation. Adaptation and direction, Sam Taylor. Camera, Karl Struss. Design, William Cameron Menzies and Laurence Irving. Editing, Allen McNeil. Sound, John Craig and David Forest. Cast: Baptista (Edwin Maxwell), Petruchio (Douglas Fairbanks), Gremio (Joseph Cawthorn), Hortensio (Geoffrey Wardwell), Grumio (Clyde Cook), Katharina (Mary Pickford), Bianca (Dorothy Jordan).

A MIDSUMMER NIGHT'S DREAM. U.S.A. 1935. Production, Warner Brothers. Direction, Max Reinhardt and William Dieterle. Script Adaptation, Charles Kenyon and Mary McCall jr. Camera, Hal Mohr, Fred Jackman, Byron Haskin, H. F. Koenekamp. Music, Felix Mendelssohn; arrangement, Erich Wolfgang Korngold. Design, Anton Grot. Choreography, Bronislava Nijinska and Nini Theilade. Editing, Ralph Dawson. Sound, Nathan Levinson. Cast: Theseus (Ian Hunter), Egeus (Grant Mitchell), Lysander (Dick Powell), Demetrius (Ross Alexander), Philostrate (Hobart Cavanaugh), Quince (Frank McHugh), Snug (Dewey Robinson), Bottom (James Cagney), Flute (Joe E. Brown), Snout (Hugh Herbert), Starveling (Otis Harlan), Hippolyta (Verree Teasdale), Hermia (Olivia de Havilland), Helena (Jean Muir), Oberon (Victor Jory), Titania (Anita Louise), Puck (Mickey Rooney), Mustardseed (Billy Barty), First Fairy (Nini Theilade), Ninny's Tomb (Arthur Treacher).

ROMEO AND JULIET. U.S.A. 1936. Production, M.G.M. Producer, Irving Thalberg. Direction, George Cukor. Adaptation, Talbot Jennings. Camera, William Daniels. Music, Herbert Stothart. Design, Cedric Gibbons, Oliver Messel, Adrian Messel. Choreography, Agnes de Mille. Editing, Margaret Booth. Cast: Escalus (Conway Tearle), Count Paris (Ralph Forbes), Montague (Robert Warwick),

155

Capulet (C. Aubrey Smith), Romeo (Leslie Howard), Mercutio (John Barrymore), Benvolio (Reginald Denny), Tybalt (Basil Rathbone), Friar Laurence (Henry Kolker), Balthasar (Maurice Murphy), Peter (Andy Devine), Lady Montague (Virginia Hammond), Lady Capulet (Violet Kemble Cooper), Juliet (Norma Shearer), Nurse (Edna May Oliver).

AS YOU LIKE IT. Great Britain 1936. Production company, Inter-Allied-Film. Production and Direction, Paul· Czinner. Adaptation, R. J. Cullen and Carl Mayer. Camera, Hal Rosson and Jack Cardiff. Music, William Walton. Design and Costumes, Lazare Meerson, John Armstrong, and Joe Strassner. Choreography, Ninette de Valois. Cast: Duke (Henry Ainley), Frederick (Felix Aylmer), Amiens (Cavin Gordon), Jaques (Leon Quartermaine), Le Beau (Austin Trevor), Charles (Lionel Braham), Oliver (John Laurie), Orlando (Laurence Olivier), Adam (Fisher White), Dennis (George More Marriott), Touchstone (Mackenzie Ward), Corin (Aubrey Mather), Silvius (Richard Ainley), William (Peter Bull), Rosalind (Elisabeth Bergner), Celia (Sophie Stewart), Phebe (Joan White), Audrey (Dorice Fordred), Lords (Cyril Horrocks, Ellis Irving, Lawrence Hanray).

HENRY V. Great Britain 1944. Production, Two Cities Films. Produced and Directed by Laurence Olivier. Adaptation, Laurence Olivier, Alan Dent, Dallas Bower. Camera, Robert Krasker, Jack Hildyard. Music, William Walton. Music direction, Muir Mathieson. Design and Costumes, Paul Sheriff, Carmen Dillon, Roger Furse. Editing, Reginald Beck. Sound, John Dennis, Desmond Dew. Technicolor. Cast: Henry V (Laurence Olivier), Gloucester (Michael Warre), Exeter (Nicholas Hannen), Salisbury (Griffith Jones), Westmoreland (Gerald Case), Archbishop of Canterbury (Felix Aylmer), Bishop of Ely (Robert Helpman), Erpingham (Morland Graham), Gower (Michael Shepley), Fluellen (Esmond Knight), MacMorris (Niall MacGinnis), Jamy (John Laurie), Bates (Arthur Hambling), Court (Brian Nissen), Williams (Jimmy Hanley), Nym (Frederick Cooper), Bardolph (Roy Emerson), Pistol (Robert Newton), Boy (George Cole), King Charles VI (Harcourt Williams), Dauphin Lewis (Max Adrian), Burgundy (Valentine Dyall), Orleans (Francis Lister), Bourbon (Russell Thorndike), Constable (Leo Genn), Harfleur (Frank Tickle), Montjoy (Jonathan Field), French Ambassador (Ernest Thesiger), Chorus (Leslie Banks), Priest (Ernest Hare), Sir John Falstaff (George Robey), Queen Isabel (Janet Burnell), Katherine (Renee Asherson), Alice (Ivy St Helier), Mistress Quickly (Freda Jackson).

HAMLET. Great Britain 1948. Production, Two Cities Films. Production and Direction, Laurence Olivier. Adaptation, Laurence Olivier and Alan Dent. Camera, Desmond Dickinson. Music, William Walton. Music direction, Muir Mathieson. Design, Carmen Dillon and Roger Furse. Editing, Helga Cranston. Sound, John Mitchell, L. E. Overton. Assistant Director, Anthony Bushell. Cast: Claudius (Basil Sydney), Hamlet (Laurence Olivier), Polonius (Felix Aylmer), Horatio (Norman Wooland), Laertes (Terence Morgan), Osric (Peter Cushing), Priest (Russell Thorndike), Marcellus (Anthony Quayle), Bernardo (Esmond Knight), Francisco (John Laurie), Captain (Niall MacGinnis), Gertrude (Eileen Herlie), Ophelia (Jean Simmons), First Player (Harcourt Williams), Second Player (Patrick Troughton), Third Player (Tony Tarver), Gravedigger (Stanley Holloway).

RICHARD III. Great Britain 1955. Production, London Film Productions. Producers, Alexander Korda, Laurence Olivier. Direction, Laurence Olivier. Adaptation, Laurence Olivier and Alan Dent. Camera, Otto Heller. Music, William Walton. Design and Costumes, Carmen Dillon and Roger Furse. Editing, Helga Cranston. Sound, Bert Rule. Vistavision-Technicolor. Cast: Edward IV (Cedric Hardwicke), Prince of Wales (Paul Huson), Young Duke of York (Andy Shine), Clarence (John Gielgud), Richard III (Laurence Olivier), Richmond (Stanley Baker), Archbishop (Nicholas Hannen), Buckingham (Ralph Richardson), Norfolk (John Philips), Rivers (Clive Morton), Dorset (Douglas Wilmer), Lord Grey (Dan Cunningham), Hastings (Alec Clunes), Stanley (Laurence Naismith), Lovel (John Laurie), Ratcliff (Esmond Knight), Catesby (Norman Wooland), Tyrrel (Patrick Troughton), Brakenbury (Andrew Cruickshank), First Priest (Russell Thorndike), Second Priest (Willoughby Gray), Lord Mayor (George Woodbridge), Queen Elizabeth (Mary Kerridge), Duchess of York (Helen Haye), Anne (Claire Bloom), Jane Shore (Pamela Brown), Page (Stewart Allen), First Monk (Wally Bascoe), Second Monk (Norman Fisher), Murderers (Michael Gough and Michael Ripper), Abbot (Roy Russell), Messenger (Peter Williams), Ostler (Timothy Bateson), Scrubwoman (Anne Wilton), Beadle (Bill Shine), Clergymen (Derek Prentice, Deering Wells), Messengers (Brian Nissen, Alexander Davion, Lane Meddick, Robert Bishop).

MACBETH. U.S.A. 1948. Production, Republic Pictures and Mercury Films. Production, Direction, Adaptation, Orson Welles. Camera, John L. Russell. Design, Fred Ritter, John McCarthy, Jnr., James Pedel. Music, Jacques Ibert. Cast: Duncan (Erskine Sanford), Malcolm (Roddy McDowall), Macbeth (Orson Welles), Banquo (Edgar Barrier), Macduff (Dan O'Herlihy), Lennox (Keene Curtis),

Ross (John Dierkes), Siward (Lionel Braham), Young Siward (Archie Heugly), Seyton (George Chirello), Doctor (Morgan Farley), Porter (Gus Schilling), Lady Macbeth (Jeanette Nolan), Gentlewoman (Laurene Tuttle), Witches (Laurene Tuttle, Brainerd Duffield, Charles Lederer), Murderers (Brainerd Duffield, William Alland), Priest (Alan Napier).

OTHELLO. Morocco 1952. Production, Mogador-Films (Mercury). Production and Direction, Orson Welles. Adaptation, Orson Welles, Jean Sacha. Camera, Anchise Brizzi, George Fanto, Obadan Troania, Roberto Fusi, G. Araldo. Music, Francesco Lavagnino, Alberto Barberis. Design, Alexander Trauner, Luigi Schiaccianoce. Costumes, Maria de Matteis. Editing, Jean Sacha, Renzo Lucidi, John Shepridge. Cast: Brabantio (Hilton Edwards), Lodovico (Nicholas Bruce), Othello (Orson Welles), Cassio (Michael Lawrence), Iago (Micheál MacLiammóir), Roderigo (Robert Coote), Montano (Jean Davis), Desdemona (Suzanne Cloutier), Emilia (Fay Compton), Bianca (Doris Dowling).

CHIMES AT MIDNIGHT. Spain-Switzerland 1965. Production, Internacional Films Espagnol, Alpine (Basel). Produced, directed and adapted by Orson Welles. Camera, Edmund Richard. Music, Alberto Lavagnino. Cast: Falstaff (Orson Welles), Hal (Keith Baxter), Henry IV (John Gielgud), Mistress Quickly (Margaret Rutherford), Doll Tearsheet (Jeanne Moreau), Henry Percy (Norman Rodway), Kate Percy (Marina Vlady), Northumberland (Fernando Rey), Justice Shallow (Alan Webb), Silence (Walter Chiari), Pistol (Michael Aldridge), Poins (Tony Beckley), Child (Beatrice Welles).

OTHELLO. U.S.S.R. 1955. Production, Mosfilm. Direction and adaptation, Sergei Yutkevitch. Camera, Evgeny Andrikanis. Design and costumes, A. Vaisfeld, V. Dorrer, M. Kariakin, O. Krochinina. Music, Aram Khachaturian. Sound, B. Volsky. Editing, B. Wolsky, Sovcolor. Cast: Othello (Sergei Bondarchuk), Desdemona (Irina Skobtseva), Iago (Andrei Popov), Cassio (Vladimir Soshalsky), Roderigo (E. Vesnik), Emilia (A. Maximova), Brabantio (E. Teterin), Doge (M. Troyanovsky), Montano (A. Kelberer), Lodovico (P. Brilling). In English language version Othello is voiced by Howard Marion Crawford, Iago by Arnold Diamond, Desdemona by Kathleen Byron, and Emilia by Nancy Nevinson.

HAMLET. U.S.S.R. 1964. Production, Lenfilm. Adaptation and Direction, Grigori Kozintsev. Translation, Boris Pasternak. Camera, I. Gritsyus. Editing, E. Makhankova. Design and costumes, E. Ene, G. Kropachev, S. Virsaladze. Music, Dmitri Shostakovich. Sound,

B. Khutoryanski. Cast: Hamlet (Innokenti Smoktunovsky), Claudius (Michail Nazwanov), Gertrude (Eliza Radzin-Szolkonis), Polonius (Y. Tolubeev), Ophelia (Anastasia Vertinskaya), Horatio (V. Erenberg), Laertes (O. Oleksenko), Guildenstern (V. Medvedev), Rosencrantz (I. Dmitriev), Fortinbras, Prince of Norway (A. Krevald), Gravedigger (V. Kolpakor), Actors (A. Chekaerskii, R. Aren, Y. Berkun), Priest (A. Lauter).

KING LEAR. U.S.S.R. 1970. Production, Lenfilm. Director, Grigori Kozintsev. Camera, Ionas Gritsus. Design, Eugene Ene. Costumes, S. Virsaladze. Editor, E. Makankova. Music, Dmitri Shostakovich. Cast: Lear (Yuri Yarvet), Goneril (Elza Radzin), Regan (Galina Volchek), Cordelia (Valentina Chendrikova), Kent (Vladimir Emelianov), Gloucester (Karl Sebris), Edgar (Leonard Merzin), Fool (Oleg Dal), Albany (Banionis).

JULIUS CAESAR. U.S.A. 1953. Production, M.G.M. Producer, John Houseman. Adaptation and Direction, Joseph L. Mankiewicz. Camera, Joseph Turrenberg. Design and Costumes, Cedric Gibbons, Edward Carfagno. Music, Miklos Rozsa. Editing, John Dunning. Cast: Julius Caesar (Louis Calhern), Antony (Marlon Brando), Cicero (Alan Napier), Brutus (James Mason), Cassius (John Gielgud), Casca (Edmond O'Brien), Flavius (Michael Pate), Marullus (George Macready), Soothsayer (Richard Hale), Decius Brutus (John Hoyt), Metellus Cimber (Tom Powers), Cinna (William Cottrell), Trebonius (Jack Raine), Ligarius (Ian Wolfe), Artemidorus (Morgan Farley), Octavius Caesar (Douglas Watson), Lepidus (Douglass Dumbrille), Lucilius (Rhys Williams), Pindarus (Michael Ansara), Messala (Dayton Lummis), Strato (Edmund Purdom), Citizens (Paul Guilfoyle, John Doucette, Lawrence Dobkin, Jo Gilbert), Calpurnia (Greer Garson), Portia (Deborah Kerr).

JULIUS CAESAR. Great Britain 1969. Production, Peter Snell for Commonwealth United. Direction, Stuart Burge. Adaptation, Robert Furnival. Camera, Ken Higgins. Design, Julia Trevelyan Oman, Maurice Pelling. Music, Michael Lewis. Editing, Eric Boyd Perkins. Cast: Antony (Charlton Heston), Brutus (Jason Robards), Julius Caesar (John Gielgud), Cassius (Richard Johnson), Casca (Robert Vaughn), Octavius Caesar (Richard Chamberlain), Portia (Diana Rigg), Calpurnia (Jill Bennett), Artemidorus (Christopher Lee), Marullus (Alan Browning), Titinius (Norman Bowler), Volumnius (Andrew Crawford), Lepidus (David Dodimead), Cinna the poet (Peter Eyre), Cinna (David Neal), Publius (Edwin Finn), Decius Brutus (Derek Godfrey), Metellus Cimber (Michael Gough), Messala (Paul Hardwick), Carpenter (Laurence Harrington), Flavius (Thomas

Heathcote), Strato (Ewan Hooper), Lucilius (Robert Keegan), Trebonius (Preston Lockwood), Popilius Lena (John Moffatt), Cicero (Andre Morell), Lucius (Steven Pacey), Cobbler (Ron Pember), Clitus (John Tate), Pindarus (Damien Thomas), Plebians (Ken Hutchinson, Michael Keating, Derek Hardwicke, Michael Wynne, David Leland).

ROMEO AND JULIET. Great Britain-Italy 1954. Production, Verona Productions, in association with Joseph Janni. Adaptation and Direction, Renato Castellani. Camera, Robert Krasker. Costume Design, Leonor Fini. Music, Roman Vlad. Editor, Sidney Hayers. Technicolor. Cast: Romeo (Laurence Harvey), Juliet (Susan Shentall), Nurse (Flora Robson), Friar Laurence (Mervyn Johns), Benvolio (Bill Travers), Tybalt (Enzo Fiermonte), Capulet (Sebastian Cabot), Mercutio (Aldo Zollo), Prince of Verona (Giovanni Rota), Lady Capulet (Lydia Sherwood), Paris (Norman Wooland), Montague (Guilio Garbinetti), Lady Montague (Nietta Zocchi), Rosaline (Dagmar Josipovich).

ROMEO AND JULIET. Great Britain-Italy 1968. Production, BHE (London), Verona Productions, Dino De Laurentiis. Producers, Anthony Havelock-Allan, John Brabourne; associate, Richard Goodwin. Adaptation, Franco Brusati, Masolino D'Amico. Direction, Franco Zeffirelli. Camera, Pasquale De Santis. Editing, Reginald Mills. Designer, Renzo Mongiardino. Costumes, Danilo Donati. Music, Nino Rota. Sound, Sash Fisher. Prologue and Epiloque spoken by Laurence Olivier. Cast: Romeo (Leonard Whiting), Juliet (Olivia Hussey), Friar Laurence (Milo O'Shea), Tybalt (Michael York), Mercutio (John McEnery), Nurse (Pat Heywood), Lady Capulet (Natasha Parry), Lord Capulet (Paul Hardwick), Prince of Verona (Robert Stephens), Balthazar (Keith Skinner), Gregory (Richard Warwick), Paris (Roberto Bisacco), Benvolio (Bruce Robinson), Lord Montague (Antonio Pierfederici), Lady Montague (Esmeralda Ruspoli), Peter (Roy Holder), Friar John (Aldo Miranda).

THE TAMING OF THE SHREW. U.S.A.-Italy 1966. Production, Richard Burton, Elizabeth Taylor, Franco Zeffirelli. Adaptation, Paul Dehn, Suso Cecchi D'Amico, Franco Zeffirelli. Camera, Oswald Morris, Luciano Trasatti. Design, John de Cuir. Music, Nino Rota. Technicolor. Cast: Petruchio (Richard Burton), Katharina (Elizabeth Taylor), Baptista (Michael Hordern), Grumio (Cyril Cusack), Lucentio (Michael York), Tranio (Alfred Lynch), Bianca (Natasha Pyne), Gremio (Alan Webb), Hortensio (Victor Spinetti), Vincentio (Mark Dignam), Priest (Giancarlo Cobelli), Pedant (Vernon Dobtcheff), Biondello (Roy Holder), Curtis (Gianni Magni), Nathaniel (Alberto

Bonucci), Gregory (Lino Capolicchio), Philip (Roberto Antonelli), Haberdasher (Anthony Garner), Tailor (Ken Parry), Widow (Bice Valori).

KUMONOSU-DJO (THE CASTLE OF THE SPIDER'S WEB): THE THRONE OF BLOOD. Japan 1957. Production, Toho. Adaptation, Akira Kurosawa, Hideo Ognuni, Shinobu Hashimoto, Ryuzo Kikushima. Direction, Akira Kurosawa. Camera, Asaichi Nakai. Music, Masaru Sato. Design, Yoshiro Murai. Editing, Akira Kurosawa. Taketoki Washizu (Macbeth, Toshiro Mifune), Asaji (Lady Macbeth, Isuzu Yamada), Kuniharu Tsuzuki (Duncan, Takamaru Sasaki), Noriyasu Odagura (Takashi Shimura), Yoshiaki Miki (Banquo, Minoru Chiaki), Yoshiteru (Fleance, Akira Kubo), Kunimaru (Malcolm, Yoichi Tachikawa), Weird Woman (Chieko Naniwa).

MACBETH. Great Britain 1960. Production, Grand Prize Films. Producer, Phil C. Samuel. Adaptation and Direction, George Schaefer. Camera, Fred A. Young. Design, Edward Carrick. Music, Richard Addinsell. Costume, Beatrice Dawson. Editing, Ralph Kemplen. Cast: Duncan (Malcolm Keen), Malcolm (Jeremy Brett), Macbeth (Maurice Evans), Lady Macbeth (Judith Anderson), Banquo (Michael Hordern), Macduff (Ian Bannen), Doctor (Felix Aylmer), Gentlewoman (Megs Jenkins), Donalbain (Barry Warren), Ross (William Hutt), Caithness (Charles Carson), Seyton (Trader Faulkner), Porter (George Rose), Witches (Valerie Taylor, Anita Sharp-Bolster, April Olrich), Angus (Brewster Mason), Menteith (Simon Lack), Fleance (Scot Finch), Sergeant (Robert Brown), Murderers (Michael Ripper, Douglas Wilmer).

THE WINTER'S TALE. Great Britain, 1966. Production, Peter Snell for Cressida/Hurst Park. Director, Frank Dunlop. Camera, Oswald Morris, Editing, Gordon Pilkington. Design, Carl Toms. Music, Jim Dale, Anthony Bowles. Cast: Leontes (Laurence Harvey), Perdita (Jane Asher), Paulina (Diana Churchill), Hermione (Moira Redmond), Autolycus (Jim Dale), Camillo (Esmond Knight), Polixenes (Richard Gale), Florizel/Archidamas (David Weston), Clown (John Gray), Old Shepherd/Gaoler (Edward Dewsbury), Steward (Michael Murray), Antigonus (Allan Foss), Emilia (Cherry Morris), Lady (Monica Maugham), Mopsa (Joy Ring), Dorcas (Joanna Wake), Lord (Dan Caulfield), Cleomines (Terry Palmer), Mamillius (Frank Barry), Shepherd Servant (Charmian Eyre).

OTHELLO. Great Britain 1965. Production, BHE. Producers, Anthony Havelock-Allan and John Brabourne; associate, Richard Goodwin. Director, Stuart Burge. Based on John Dexter's stage production for the National Theatre. Camera, Geoffrey Unsworth. Design, William Kellner (stage designer, Jocelyn Herbert). Editing, Richard Marden. Technicolor. Cast: Othello (Laurence Olivier), Desdemona (Maggie Smith), Iago (Frank Finlay), Emilia (Joyce Redman), Cassio (Derek Jacobi), Roderigo (Robert Lang), Lodovico (Kenneth Mackintosh), Brabantio (Anthony Nicholls), Bianca (Sheila Reid), Gratiano (Michael Turner), Montano (Edward Hardwicke), Doge (Harry Lomax), Clown (Roy Holder).

A MIDSUMMER NIGHT'S DREAM. Great Britain 1969. Production, Royal Shakespeare Company and Alan Clore. Producer, Michael Birkett. Direction, Peter Hall. Camera, Peter Suschitzky. Editing, Jack Harris. Design and Costumes, John Bury, Ann Curtis. Music, Guy Wolfenden. Eastman Colour. Cast: Theseus (Derek Godfrey), Hippolyta (Barbara Jefford), Philostrate (Hugh Sullivan), Egeus (Nicholas Selby), Lysander (David Warner), Demetrius (Michael Jayston), Helena (Diana Rigg), Hermia (Helen Mirren), Oberon (Ian Richardson), Titania (Judi Dench), Puck (Ian Holm), Bottom (Paul Rogers), Quince (Sebastian Shaw), Snout (Bill Travers), Flute (John Normington), Snug (Clive Swift), Starveling (Donald Eccles).

HAMLET. Great Britain 1969. Production, Woodfall. Direction, Tony Richardson. Camera, Gerry Fisher. Art Direction, Jocelyn Herbert. Editing, Charles Rees. Cast: Hamlet (Nicol Williamson), Claudius (Anthony Hopkins), Gertrude (Judy Parfitt), Polonius (Mark Dignam), Ophelia (Marianne Faithfull), Laertes (Michael Pennington), Horatio (Gordon Jackson), Rosencrantz (Ben Aris), Guildenstern (Clive Graham), Osric (Peter Gale), Marcellus/Player King (John Carney), Barnardo/Player/Sailor (John Trenaman), Francisco/Courtier/Player (Robin Chadwick), Player Queen/Courtier (Richard Everett), Lucianus/Gravedigger (Roger Livesey), Sailor/ Courtier (John Railton), Reynaldo/Courtier/Player (Roger Lloyd-Pack), Captain/Courtier (Michael Epphick), Courtier (Bill Jarvis), Priest/Courtier (Ian Collier), Court Ladies (Jennifer Tudor, Angelica Huston), Messenger/Courtier (Mark Griffith).

KING LEAR. Denmark, 1969–70. First shown 1971. Production, Athena-Laterna Films. Producer, Michael Birkett. Director, Peter Brook. Camera, Henning Kristiansen. Design, Georges Wakhevitch. Costumes, Adele Anggård. Sound, Robert Allen. Editing, Albert Jurgenson. Cast: King Lear (Paul Scofield), Goneril (Irene Worth), Regan (Susan Engel), Cordelia (Anne-Lise Gabold), Duke of Cornwall (Patrick Magee), Duke of Albany (Cyril Cusack), Earl of Kent (Tom Fleming), Earl of Gloucester (Alan Webb), Edmund (Ian Hogg), Edgar (Robert Lloyd), Fool (Jack MacGowran), Oswald (Barry Stanton).

Selected Bibliography

Included are a few recent books out of many on Shakespeare and the plays which have proved of special use in the preparation of this volume.

AICKEN, FREDERICK, 'Shakespeare on the Screen', *Screen Education*, September–October 1963.

BALL, ROBERT HAMILTON, *Shakespeare on Silent Film*. London, Allen and Unwin, 1968.

BARKER, FELIX, *The Oliviers: a Biography*. London, Hamish Hamilton, 1953.

BILLARD, PIERRE, 'Chimes at Midnight', *Sight and Sound*, British Film Institute, Spring 1965.

BIRKETT, MICHAEL, 'King Lear: from Page to Screen', *Journal of the Society for Film and Television Arts*, Autumn 1969.

BLUMENTHAL, J., 'Macbeth into Throne of Blood', *Sight and Sound*, British Film Institute, Autumn 1965.

BROOK, PETER, 'Shakespeare on Three Screens', *Sight and Sound*, British Film Institute, Spring 1965.

BROWN, IVOR, *How Shakespeare Spent the Day*. London, the Bodley Head, 1963.

COWIE, PETER, *The Cinema of Orson Welles*. London, Zwemmer, 1965.

CROSS, BRENDA (editor), *The Film Hamlet*. London, The Saturn Press, 1948.

DEHN, PAUL, 'The Filming of Shakespeare', in *Talking of Shakespeare*, edited by John Garrett. London, Hodder & Stoughton, 1954.

DENT, ALAN (editor), *Hamlet: the Film and the Play*. London, World Film Publications, 1948.

Furse, Roger, 'The Middle Ages through Modern Eyes', *Films and Filming*, April-May 1955.

—'A Wardrobe for *Richard III*', *Films and Filming*, April–May 1955.

Griffin, A., 'Shakespeare through the Camera's Eye', *Shakespeare Quarterly*, New York, No. 4, 1953, No. 6, 1955, No. 7, 1956.

Hall, Peter, 'Why the Fairies Have Dirty Faces', the *Sunday Times*, London, 26 January 1969.

—'On the Dank and Dirty Ground', *Journal of the Society of Film and Television Arts*, Autumn 1969.

Halliday, F. E., *The Life of Shakespeare*. London, Duckworth, revised edition 1964.

Hamlet (film); 'The Play and the Screenplay', *Hollywood Quarterly*, Spring 1948.

Hamlet (film). *Fiches Filmographiques*, No. 17. IDHEC (Institut des Hautes Études Cinématographiques), Paris.

Harbage, A. B., *Shakespeare's Audience*. New York, Columbia University Press, 1941.

—*Theatre for Shakespeare*. University of Toronto Press, 1955.

Hayman, Ronald, 'Shakespeare on the Screen', *Times Literary Supplement*, 26 September 1968. London.

Henry V (film). *Fiches Filmographiques*, No. 50. IDHEC, Paris.

Herrold, Leonard. 'Notes on Macbeth', *Sight and Sound*, British Film Institute, March 1950.

Houseman, John, 'On Filming Julius Caesar', *Films in Review*, April 1953. New York.

Huntley, John, 'The Music of Hamlet', *Penguin Film Review*, No. 8, 1949. London, Penguin Books.

Hutton, C. Clayton, *The Making of Henry V*. London, privately published in 1944.

—*Macbeth; the Making of the Film*. London, Max Parrish, 1960.

Isaacs, J., *Production and Stage Management at the Blackfriars Theatre*. London University Press, 1946.

Johnson, Ian, 'Merely Players—400 Years of Shakespeare', *Films and Filming*, April 1964.

Joseph, B. L., *Elizabethan Acting*. Oxford University Press, 1951.

Julius Caesar (film). Article in *Hollywood Quarterly*, Winter 1953.

Julius Caesar (film). Jules César. *Fiches Filmographiques*, No. 92, IDHEC, Paris.

KELLY, F. M., *Shakespearean Costume for Stage and Screen*. London, A. and C. Black, 1970.

KOTT, JAN, *Shakespeare Our Contemporary*. London, Methuen, 1964.

KOZINTSEV, Grigori, 'The Hamlet Within Me'; *Films and Filming*, September 1962.

— *Shakespeare: Time and Conscience*. London, Dobson, 1967.

KUROSAWA, AKIRA. Interview by T. Sato. *Journal of the Society of Film and Television Arts*, London, Autumn 1969.

KUSTOW, MICHAEL, A review of Kozintsev's *Shakespeare: Time and Conscience*, *Sight and Sound*, British Film Institute, Summer 1968.

LALOU, RENÉ, 'Shakespeare, Précurseur du Cinéma', *L'Âge Nouveau*, No. 109, April–June 1960. Paris.

LILLICH, MEREDITH, 'Shakespeare on the Screen', *Films in Review*, June–July 1956. New York.

MacLIAMMÓIR, MICHEAL. *Put Money in Thy Purse: a Diary of the Film of Othello*. London, Methuen, 1952.

MANVELL, ROGER, 'Shakespeare as a Scriptwriter', *World Review*, May 1952. New York.

— 'The Film of Hamlet', *Penguin Film Review*, No. 8, 1949. London, Penguin Books.

— (editor), 'Shakespeare on the Screen', special issue of the *Journal of the Society of Film and Televison Arts*. No. 37, Autumn 1969.

— and HUNTLEY, JOHN, *The Technique of Film Music*. London, the Focal Press, 1957.

MORRIS, PETER, *Shakespeare on Film. An Index*. Ottawa, 1964.

NOBLE, PETER, *The Fabulous Orson Welles*. London, Hutchinson, 1956.

OLIVIER, Sir LAURENCE, 'Filming Shakespeare', *Journal of the British Film Academy*, Autumn, 1955.

Othello (film). *Fiches Filmographiques*, No. 147. IDHEC, Paris.

PASTERNAK, BORIS, 'On Translating Shakespeare', *Cinema Nuovo*, No. 132, 1958. Rome.

PHILLIPS, JAMES E. 'Adapted from a Play by Shakespeare', *Hollywood Quarterly*, October 1946.

— 'By William Shakespeare—with Additional Dialogue', *Hollywood Quarterly*, Spring 1951.

PROUSE, DEREK. Review of Yutkevitch's film of *Othello* in *Sight and Sound*, British Film Institute, Summer 1956.

RAYNOR, HENRY, 'Shakespeare Filmed', *Sight and Sound*, British Film Institute, July–September 1952.

REDI, RICCARDO, and CHITI, ROBERTO, 'Shakespeare e il Cinema: Filmografia', *Bianco e Nero*, January 1957. Rome.

Romeo and Juliet (film). *Fiches Filmographiques*, No. 120. IDHEC, Paris.

ROWSE, A. L., *William Shakespeare*. London, Macmillan, 1963.

SATO, TADAO, 'Japanese "Macbeth"', *Journal of the Society of Film and Television Arts*. Autumn 1969.

SAVILLE, PHILIP, 'Record of a Television Production' [*Hamlet*]; *Journal of the Society of Film and Television Arts*, Autumn 1969.

Shakespeare im Film. Deutsches Institut für Filmkunde. 1964.

'Shakespeare in the Mass Media', articles in *Hollywood Quarterly*, Nos 2, 3 and 4, 1953, 1954.

SHAKESPEARE, WILLIAM, *Romeo and Juliet. A Motion Picture Edition*. Script of the M.G.M. film of 1936. London, Arthur Barker, n.d.

TAYLOR, JOHN RUSSELL, Article on Shakespearean film in *Shakespeare: a Celebration*, edited by J. J. B. Spencer. London, Pelican Books, 1964.

TIRUCHELVAM, SHARMINI. 'Encounter on the Field of Philippi'. The *Daily Telegraph Magazine*, 6th February 1970.

TUCKER, NICHOLAS, 'Shakespeare and Film Technique'; *Screen Education*, September–October 1963.

WAIN, JOHN, *The Living World of Shakespeare*. London, Macmillan, 1964. Reissue in Pelican Books, 1966.

WELLES, ORSON, 'The Third Audience', *Sight and Sound*, British Film Institute, January–March 1954.

— Interview of, by André Bazin and others, in *Cahiers du Cinema*, No. 87, September 1958.

WHITEHEAD, PETER, and BEAN, ROBIN, *Olivier: Shakespeare*. London, Lorrimer Films Limited, 1966.

YUTKEVITCH, SERGEI, 'Othello', *Cinéma '56*. March–April 1956.

— 'My Way with Shakespeare', *Films and Filming*, October 1957.

Index

McDowall, Roddy, 59
MacLiammóir, Micheál, 55, 61–2
Magnani, Anna, 122
Mankiewicz, Joseph, 9; film version of *Julius Caesar* (1953), 86–91, 92–3, 95, 124, 133, 153
Mark, John, 31
Marlowe, Christopher, 12, 52
Marowitz, Charles, 135
Mason, James, 91, 93
Mathieson, Muir, 46
Matthews, A. E., 19
Mayer, Carl, 31
Meerson, Lazare, 31
Méliès, Georges, 17
Menzies, William Cameron, 24
Mendelssohn, Felix, 26–7, 123, 127
Merchant of Venice, The, 18, 19, 20, 21, 22, 131
Merry Wives of Windsor, The, 64
Messel, Oliver, 32
Midgley, Robin, 131
Midsummer Night's Dream, A, 8, 18, 21, 155; film version by Max Reinhardt and William Dieterle (1934), 25–7, 35; by Peter Hall (1969), 119–27, 136, 138, 142, 154
Mifune, Toshiro, 102 et seq.
Moorehead, Agnes, 59
Morley, Royston, 131
Morley, Sheridan, 132
Mounet, Paul, 18
Mounet-Sully (Jean Sully Mounet), 18

National Film Archive (Great Britain), 22
National Theatre of Great Britain, 117, 141
Nazwanov, Michail, 129
Nielsen, Asta, 21
Nijinska, Bronislava, 26
Neumann, Hans, 21
Neuss, Alwin, 18
Noble, Peter, 61
Noh drama (Japan), 101 et seq., 112–13

Nolan, Jeanette, 59–60
Nunn, Trevor, 52

O'Brien, Edmond, 87
O'Ferrall, George More, 131
O'Herlihy, Dan, 59
O'Shea, Milo, 99
Olivier, Laurence (Lord Olivier), 9, 15, 16, 30, 31, 35, 36, 37–54, 89, 92, 98, 106, 107, 114, 117–20, 133, 153; film version of *Henry V* (1944), 16, 35, 37–40, 52–3, 64, 89, 106, 131, 142; of *Hamlet* (1948), 35, 40–7, 53–4, 89, 119; of *Richard III* (1955), 2, 15, 35, 47–51, 54, 115; project for *Macbeth*, 51; appearance in film version of *Othello* (1965), 117–119, 153
Othello, 4, 9, 15, 18, 131; film version by Dmitri Buchowetzki (1922), 3, 22; by Orson Welles (1952), 60–4, 70, 106, 133; by Sergei Yutkevitch (1955), 73–7; by Stuart Burge (1965), 92, 117–19, 153

Padovani, Lea, 61
Pasternak, Boris, 13, 72, 79, 153
Pickford, Mary, 23–5, 35
Phillips, James E., 52
Plumb, E. Hay, 20
Plummer, Christopher, 9, 131
Plutarch, 11
Popov, Andrei, 74
Porten, Henny, 21
Powell, Dick, 26, 27

Quartermaine, Leon, 31

Rank, J. Arthur (Lord Rank), 47, 51
Ranous, William V., 18
Rathbone, Basil, 32
Rathbone, Mrs Basil, 19
Raymond, Charles, 19
Real Thing at Last, The (burlesque of *Macbeth* by James Bridie, 1914), 19

Redmond, Moira, 116
Reed, Sir Carol, 48
Reinhardt, Max, 8, 25–7, 127
Richard II, 64, 131
Richard III, 18, 131; version by
  Sir Frank Benson (1911), 19, 22,
  114; by Laurence Olivier (1955),
  2, 15, 35, 47–51, 54, 115
Richardson, Sir Ralph, 65
Richardson, Tony, 119; version of
  Hamlet (1969), 127–30
Robards, Jason, 93–4, 96
Robson, Dame Flora, 98
Rodolfi, Eleuterio, 20
Romeo and Juliet, 9, 18, 19, 20, 131;
  version by George Cukor (1936),
  9, 28–30, 32, 37, 38; version by
  Renato Castellani (1954), 97–8;
  by Franco Zeffirelli (1968), 98–9
Rooney, Mickey, 27
Round House (London), 127 et seq.
Royal Shakespeare Company, 117,
  126, 131, 140
Royal Shakespeare Enterprises, 119
Rozsa, Miklos, 95
Ruggeri, Ruggero, 20

Sato, Tadao, 102 et seq.
Saville, Philip, 131
Schaefer, George, film version of
  Macbeth (1960), 115–16
Schall, Heinz, 21
Scofield, Paul, 93, 117, 135, 140,
  143
Shakespeare, William, origin of
  Shakespearean scholarship in
  18th century, 1–2; working life
  of, 2, 3 et seq.; 20th-century
  approach to, 2; silent film versions of plays, 3; Elizabethan
  theatre conditions, 5–6; idiom and
  vocabulary, 6–7; contemporary
  nature of his writing for us, 7;
  bad tradition of acting in plays,
  7–8; range of interpretation of,
  8–9; the film-makers' approach
  to plays, 9 et seq.; and on television, 9; handling of sources,
11; response to audience taste
  of his times, 12; vandalism in
  handling of text; 13; in translation and foreign adaptation,
  13–14; relation of sight to sound,
  14; relation of Elizabethan stage
  technique to film technique, 14–
  15; silent film versions of plays,
  17–22; appeal of plays to Russian
  intelligentsia, 72; political
  thought in plays, 86
Shakespeare: Time and Conscience
  (Grigori Kozintsev), 77 et seq.
Shakespeare Writing Julius Caesar
  (Georges Méliès, 1907), 18
Shaw, G. Bernard, 4, 32–4, 114
Shearer, Norma, 28, 30, 38
Shentall, Susan, 30, 98
Shostakovich, Dimitri, 79, 85
Shylock, ou le More de Venise (1913),
  19
Sinden, Donald, 131
Skanderbeg (Sergei Yutkevitch), 72
Snell, Peter, 91 et seq., 116–17
Spiegel, Sam, 51
Spread of the Eagle, The, 131
Suschitzky, Peter, 127
Sydney, Basil, 129

Taming of the Shrew, The, 8, 19;
  version by D. W. Griffith (1908),
  18; by Sam Taylor (1929), 23–5;
  by Franco Zeffirelli (1966), 99–
  100
Taylor, Elizabeth, 99–100
Taylor, John Russell, 27
Taylor, Sam, 23–5
Tearle, Godfrey, 19
Television, Shakespeare on, 120 et
  seq., 131, 131–2
Tempest, The, 17
Terry, Ellen, 30
Thalberg, Irving G., 28, 32
Thanhouser, Edwin, 18, 20
Theilade, Nini, 26
Tiruchelvam, Sharmini, 96
Titus Andronicus, 12
Toida, Michizo, 102